THE TEST BOOK

Also by Krogerus/Tschäppeler:

The Decision Book – Fifty Models for Strategic Thinking
The Change Book – Fifty Models to Explain How Things Happen
The Question Book

www.rtmk.ch

MIKAEL KROGERUS

ROMAN TSCHÄPPELER

THE TEST BOOK

64 TOOLS TO LEAD YOU TO SUCCESS

Assistance: Cédric Hiltbrand

With illustrations by Carla Schmid

Translated by Jenny Piening

PROFILE BOOKS

First published in Great Britain in 2014 by
Profile Books Ltd
3a Exmouth House
Pine Street
London
EC1R 0JH

First published in Switzerland, entitled
Das Testbuch
by Kein und Aber AG Zurich
www.keinundaber.ch

1 3 5 7 9 10 8 6 4 2

Printed and bound in Italy by L.E.G.O S.p.a Lavis

ISBN 9781781253205
eISBN 9781782830948

CONTENTS

Put to the test

WHAT IT'S ABOUT

Never before have humans had to undergo as many tests as today. There's a test before it all starts (a pregnancy test) and one when it's all over (a test to determine the cause of death). And in between? From the cradle to the grave, from head to toe, we're subjected to a barrage of evaluations, standardisations and formulae: prenatal diagnostics, PISA, GCSEs, driving test, army physical, IQ, EQ, fitness test, depression test, dementia test – life is one long test, and we are just the candidates.

WHAT YOU WILL FIND IN THIS BOOK

We have compiled sixty-four tests – famous and obscure ones, historical and brand-new ones – that interpret your life. You can do some of the tests right away (Am I in the right job? How well do I know my partner? Do I drink too much?). Others give you a taster and tips on what to do if push comes to shove (polygraph, Rorschach test, GMAT). In every case you will find out about the test's origins, how it is evaluated and what the result reveals about you.

Don't expect any tests that assess machines, products or methods – the tests in this book are to do with you and your life. And don't expect any gossip-magazine horoscopes; the tests are (on the whole) reliable and based on scientific testing methods. What you can look forward to is tests that are fun and quick to do, and that might produce some surprising – or thought-provoking – results.

WHAT IS A TEST

A test is a measurement method. A basic distinction can be made between binary, quantitative and qualitative tests. Binary tests divide results into two categories: positive-negative, right–wrong, pregnant–not pregnant. Quantitative tests locate your result on a scale and compare it to other people's results, for example IQ tests or sport tests. Qualitative tests produce descriptive, typological results, like the MBTI®. But tests are also powerful instruments. They decide who belongs and who doesn't. They draw the line between normal and crazy, between us and others, between below and above average.

2 HOW TO USE THIS BOOK

You can open this book at any page and dip in and out as you please. Test yourself, your friends, colleagues or family members. *The Test Book* is written for anyone who is curious. Because tests don't only serve the purpose of compartmentalising, they also provide orientation: Who am I? What can I do? Where do I stand in comparison to others? Only when you know where you stand, can you find out where you want to go.

GETTING STARTED

If you are more practically minded and want to start by evaluating your own life, then go straight to the first test on page 10. Or if you want to first find out about the origins of testing, begin overleaf with the prologue, 'A brief history of the test'.

A brief history of the test

Tests are as old as humanity, and there are four fundamental questions that we have never stopped asking: 'Are you guilty?', 'Are you able?', 'Who am I?' and 'Am I sick?'.

We all know the guilt question from the Bible. In the guise of a wily snake, God tested whether Adam and Eve could resist the temptation of the apple. They couldn't. In the Book of Numbers we find the famous infidelity test: a wife whose husband suspects her of adultery is made to drink a potion of bitter water. Her 'belly swelling and thigh falling' was proof of her guilt. A psychologically convincing lie test can be traced back to early India. The suspected liar is led into a dark tent. Inside there is a donkey, whose tail has been coated in lamp oil. The man is told to pull on the donkey's tail. If he is a liar, the man is told, pulling the donkey's tail will cause it to scream, because it is clairvoyant. The man is left alone with the animal and after a while brought back out of the tent. It doesn't matter if the donkey screamed or not, the evidence is on the man's hands. If they are clean it proves his guilt as he didn't touch the donkey's tail, and according to the inventors of this test, you can tell a liar by his fear of being found out. Modern lie detector tests are based on the same principle (→ Polygraph Test and Reid® Method, p. 30)

DIVINE JUDGEMENT

The very first documented test in human history also dealt with the question of guilt. Divine judgement was a well-known method for establishing guilt in ancient China, India and Asia Minor. To establish the accused person's guilt, he had to 'go before God'. One of the oldest written records, the Code of Ur-Nammu (2100 BC) describes such divine judgements. For example, in the 'ordeal by water' the accused is thrown into water; if he drowned, he was guilty. This method continued to be used for thousands of years, albeit in many variations. In the witch trials in the Middle Ages in Europe, for example, the 'trial by water' was interpreted the other way round. If the woman didn't drown, she was guilty, if she did drown she was innocent (but unfortunately dead).

INITIATION AND ASSESSMENT

'Are you guilty?' is the first question that tests have dealt with since time immemorial. The second is 'Are you able?' We know from early documentation of initiation rites, trials of courage and inauguration ceremonies that joining a community often involved passing a test. Before being accepted into a group, the aspirant, or novice, first had to prove himself to the community. Little has changed: from religious communities to fraternities, indigenous tribes to street gangs, becoming a member involves passing a test. In the USA, if you want to join one of the powerful frats (fraternities), you have to go through a 'hazing' ritual, the unofficial admission test. In Dartmouth College, for example, candidates have to eat a 'vomelet' (an omelette made of vomit). And those who want to join the white supremacist prison gang the Aryan Brotherhood, have to kill a fellow prison inmate. After being circumcised, Maasai boys have to set up a camp deep in the bush and live there for ten years with other freshly circumcised boys before returning to the community. And those who want a Christian baptism have to first spend a year proving their faith.

The idea of judging humans based on merit rather than heredity originated in China. Around AD 600, the Sui dynasty established the *kēju*, or imperial examinations, for recruiting bureaucrats – a mixture of army physical, rote learning and little puzzles. For example, in the final exam, candidates had to drink strong liquor and then compose a poem – which isn't hard to imagine as a creative exercise in some modern assessment centres.

THE PSYCHOTECHNICIANS

In the western world, the idea that a young person would choose a career based on a job-oriented test rather than on family tradition or personal inclination, is a relatively new phenomenon. It started at the beginning of the 20th century and was inspired by machine efficiency testing. The American Frederick Winslow Taylor ('Taylorism') searched for the optimal working process that eliminated every imprecision, every inefficiency, every unnecessary motion. Because it worked so well with machines, in the 1920s the 'psychotechnician' asked himself: Why not do the same with humans? It was assumed that particular skills were necessary for particular working processes, but that these could not be learned. Instead, they were ascertained in an aptitude test, the results of which allocated candidates a particular job. The 900-page standard reference work *Handbuch Psychotechnischer Eignungsprüfungen (Handbook of Psychotechnical Aptitude Tests)* by Fritz Giese from 1925 reveals the breadth of these kinds of tests. The job aptitudes range from 'female hand coordination skills' to the 'suitcase test', in which you had to pack a case with clothes and 'unwieldy objects'.

In the mid-1950s such aptitude tests were replaced by the kind of testing we are familiar with today. Nowadays, a person is hired not because she can prove that she is able to carry out a particular work process, but because she is the best person for the job.

MODERN ORACLE

The third big test question is 'Who am I?' When you were at your wit's end in Ancient Greece, you would consult an oracle. The most famous and popular oracle was the one in Delphi – despite or because of the fact that instead of giving clear answers, it would recite enigmatic verses that usually only made sense once the future had come to pass. Over the entrance to the temple of Delphi where the oracle lived, there was an inscription: *Gnothi seauthon* ('Know Thyself').

This maxim is important. It is the leitmotif running through all attempts to measure a person's soul, personality and temperament. The entire history of tests can be seen as an attempt to give scientific credence to the ancient oracle.

The first attempt at describing a person based on his personality (and not on his physical features or his heredity), was made in ancient Greece. The result was the four temperaments: choleric, melancholic, phlegmatic and sanguine (→ Temperament Test, p. 10).

It would be another 2,000 years until the next serious attempt was made to quantify the personality of a human being. The Swiss pastor Johann Caspar Lavater developed an idea already suggested by Aristotle, that it was possible to judge a person's character and intelligence based on hair colour, brain size, bone structure or nose shape. Physiognomy enjoyed its heyday in the 19th and early 20th centuries and served as a basis for eugenics and racist ideology.

These kinds of interpretations were countered by Sigmund Freud's exploration of the psyche. According to his revolutionary theory, our personality is not just innate, but is also shaped by our culture. In 1921, Freud's former pupil Carl Gustav Jung published his work *Psychological Types*, creating a classification system that is still used today. In his book, Jung defined two 'attitudes': extroverted and introverted. People show their true selves in their behaviour towards the outside world: extroverts focus on other people and the outside world, introverts focus inwards on their own thoughts and feelings. Your personality type is determined by the combination of these attitudes with four 'functions' – thinking, feeling, sensing and intuition – which each individual uses with a varying amount of success and frequency. Jung used historic figures to illustrate his types, so for example, Goethe was 'extrovert and intuitive', somebody 'who always sees new possibilities and who in his eternal striving for change tears down what he has only just built'. However, Jung was aware of the limitations of such sketchy classifications. The true complexity of a person can never be fully described.

WHO AM I? AND HOW GOOD AM I?

Personality classifications were originally conceived as clinical instruments, but by the mid-20th century, human resources had discovered the possibilities of using typologies during the recruitment process. One example of this is the scientifically controversial yet still widely used MBTI® (→ Myers-Briggs Type Indicator, p. 42). This test judges a person in the Jungian tradition according to how he presents himself to the outside world. This involves questions such as: Are you more of a practical or effusive person? Is it more important for you to stick to your principles or to listen to your feelings? It is usually easy to answer spontaneously, but if you take time to think about it, you will usually come to the conclusion that the only real answer is 'It depends'. Because in some situations you might be goal-oriented and pragmatic, in others dreamy

and distracted. Which brings us to one of the most frequent criticisms of such methods: their binary nature. You have to be either introverted *or* extroverted, thinking *or* feeling. There are no grey areas and therefore no ambivalence.

And yet it would be a mistake to write off these kinds of tests completely. The business journalist Malcolm Gladwell showed how they are both banal *and* very clever. As a student he developed his own test with a friend, asking the following questions:

1. In a romantic relationship are you more canine or feline? (In other words: are you the pursuer, who runs happily to the door, tail wagging? Or are you the pursued?)
2. Information: Do you need a lot of or specific information? (In other words: Do you want to know everything there is to know about something, or are you satisfied with vague information to stimulate your imagination?)
3. Are you an insider or an outsider? (In other words: Do you have a good relationship with your parents, or do you define yourself outside of the relationship to your parents?)
4. Are you a nibbler or a gobbler? (Do you work steadily, in small increments, or do everything at once, in a big gulp?)

The four questions cover the areas

of relationships, cognition, family and work habits. The test is of course nonsense. Yet you immediately recognise yourself – and others.

In modern psychology, the 'Big Five' model is the standard means of categorising personality types (→ Big Five Test, p. 18). This test is also criticised for asking too little with too many questions. But at least its five personality types are not exclusively binary, but scaled. You are both one thing and another, not one or the other. But progress is being made here, too: The 2.0 version of the Big Five Test is the 'One-Click-Personality', software developed by David Stillwell and Michal Kosinski at Cambridge University, which registers all pages, comments and posts that you 'like' on your Facebook page. Based on this data it produces a Big Five personality profile and compares it with a 'norm group', your Facebook friends. If it's true that our private lives are increasingly taking place online through social media, this kind of typing could supersede traditional psychological questionnaires in terms of accuracy. Websites like youarewhatyoulike.com or labs.five.com already work with this theory.

THE SCREW-UP THAT I AM

Modern personality tests reveal an important shift in testing: aptitude tests or psychological assessments were prescribed by the powers that be, but nowadays we usually carry out personality and performance tests off our own bat. The willingness with which we evaluate our talent, our work-life balance, our sex life, our spiritual potential or our risk tolerance using tests, questionnaires and checklists on the Internet, in magazines or in books like this one, is not only an expression of the old longing to know oneself. Above all, it points to our deep-rooted insecurity. Could I have done better in life? To take it to the extreme, you could say that the question 'Who am I?' has been replaced with the self-optimising question 'Am I good enough?' We assess ourselves and compare ourselves to others, we conceal our weaknesses and emphasise our strengths. At their core, most tests are about inferring future performance, risks, intentions or possibilities from the past (career, medical history, buying behaviour) and from comparisons with others (norm group, target group, circle of friends). It is this 'prognostic validity', i.e. the promise of an alleged predictability of events, which make tests so attractive.

THE FUTURE OF THE TEST

Our obsession with analysing ourselves is not just restricted to our personalities or careers, but is increasingly also extending to our physical performance. Self tracking, i.e. recording every kind of imaginable personal data – from calorie consumption to blood pressure to the number of steps we take a day – is an indication of how we have come to concentrate obsessively on ourselves. The writer Juli Zeh wrote that biocentric is egocentric. The human is nothing more than a constantly self-evaluating and judging candidate; the norm that we compare ourselves to is our Facebook friends. At the same time, self-tracking apps represent a shift towards the fourth big test question: Am I healthy? The decisive question is no longer 'How good am I?' but 'How am I?' Of course, health has always been an important issue, as we know from the ancient Egyptian 'Smith Papyrus' (approx. 1500 BC), probably the world's first medical text. But historically, knowing if you were healthy or ill was a question that could only be answered by experts. Today, apps facilitate self-diagnosis.

The next generation of self-tracking apps not only collates specific values, but also analyses our metadata: Where am I, with whom, since when, for how long? Our every movement, what we eat and drink, our feelings and reactions, are measured, compared and evaluated. And one day, apps will also be able to tell us what we have gained – financially, emotionally and in terms of our health – from our contacts, jobs and activities. Some people believe that 'life tracking' is just a step behind gene tracking (→ Gene Test, p. 82). But we don't just test ourselves and our offspring; we are constantly passing judgement on everything and everyone around us: a professor's lecture, the book we bought on Amazon, the service in the hotel, the advice of a financial advisor, the candidates on a talent show, the posts of our friends. And we immediately publish our 'score' in the form of online comments. We live in a data dictatorship, our ideology is measurability. And tests are the oracle of the modern world.

Personality & character

10

Am I a choleric?

WHAT IT'S ABOUT

When it comes down to it, people care about two things: understanding themselves and being understood by others. We strive for self-awareness and long for people to see us as we really are.

THE TEST

The first person to try and explain 'who we really are' was the philosopher Empedocles (490–430 BC). He compared the temperaments of different people with the characteristics of the four elements – fire, water, earth and air. Some people are hot-headed like fire, others as gentle as water. The four elements also corresponded to particular gods: Earth (Hera) is phlegmatic but constant, water (Persephone) gentle but deep, air (Hermes) exuberant but volatile, and fire (Zeus) determined but choleric. Galen of Pergamon linked this approach to Hippocrates' humoral pathology and coined the terms choleric, melancholic, phlegmatic and sanguine.

HOW IT'S EVALUATED

The four designations are still in common use today, and although it is hard to pin down their precise meaning, we can usually intuitively find an example of each among our colleagues. The choleric, whose fire flares up and abates without providing warmth; the sanguine one, who is vivacious but jumps erratically from one thing to another; the melancholic, who is a burden to himself; and the phlegmatic, who is a burden to others. Seen in the light of modern psychology, the four temperaments and their hybrid forms have become obsolete. And yet they form the historic foundation for the way in which we define human characteristics, and are deeply rooted in popular culture.

GOOD TO KNOW

Your temperament comes to the fore when you feel like you have been treated unfairly. Your character is revealed in the way you treat people from whom you have nothing to gain.

Evaluate these statements on a scale of 1 to 5:

doesn't apply to me at all   1 — 2 — 3 — 4 — 5   completely applies to me

....

1. You are bursting with childish energy and optimism, and you like to gesticulate when you speak.

2. You wear your heart on your sleeve and never hide your feelings. In an animated conversation you have no problem gripping or touching the other person's arm.

3. You have a knack for storytelling and others enjoy listening to you. You inspire others and make them laugh.

4. You find it easy to win people over with your charm and wit, and you rarely need facts to do so.

5. In conversation you are more of a talker than a listener. What you want to say is so important to you that you sometimes interrupt the person you are talking to.

6. From one minute to the next, your mood can change from elated to gloomy.

7. You are overhasty, easily distracted and quick to get bored. You find it hard to develop routines and rhythms, although you know it would be good for you.

8. You want to feel loved and need to be popular and applauded. You allow a lot, and do everything, to be liked.

....

9. You prefer to make a plan and to follow it. You are better at developing and making a plan than carrying it out.

10. You are methodical, organised and tidy. You like detailed work. Maths, research, controlling expenditure, handicrafts, and graphic design are areas in which you might feel at home.

11. You are quick to recognise the feelings and needs of others. You are in tune with your own and others' feelings.

12. You have an intense, deep personality. You are prone to introspection and enjoy deep conversations with one other person. You hate superficial chit-chat.

13. It is hard to please you. You bear grudges.

14. You try and see the good side of things and to stay positive, but quickly see the difficult side of a situation.

15. You often withdraw and need a lot of time to yourself. You are happy with your own company.

16. Wherever you are, whatever you're doing: you are constantly analysing and judging situations, other people and yourself.

....

17. 'I agree!' is a sentence that you often come out with. You rarely feel the need to assert yourself or your opinions. You are adaptable.

18. You are tactful, sensitive and polite with others.

19. You are balanced, calm and collected. You are unperturbed by delays and hectic situations. You are patient, easy-going and tolerant.

20. You have a dry sense of humour, which is expressed in sarcastic comments but always with a twinkle in your eye.

21. You find it hard to make decisions.

22. You are laid-back and rarely swept away by anything. You measure activities with the equation: gain divided by effort.

23. You are often unsure, worry, and mull over problems alone.

24. You avoid conflict. Anger and frustration eat into you.

....

25. You love a challenge. You see it as an opportunity to show what you're capable of. You turn every situation into a competition.

26. You are assertive and sure of yourself. People think twice before speaking out against you.

27. You don't care what other people think of you or your ideas, you are confident of your own abilities.

28. You are decisive. In almost all situations you act quickly and efficiently.

29. You are impatient with others. You react over-hastily, irritably and impetuously. You are bad at accepting other points of view or ways of working.

30. You find it difficult to show feelings and affection.

31. Your persistence can quickly turn to stubbornness.

32. You are a workaholic. You are spurred on by the fact that you feel unhappy or even worthless if you are not constantly doing or achieving something.

....

Add up your points and insert them in the table below.

Which type is most pronounced in you? For which type did you get the fewest points? Ask somebody who knows you well to fill out the table for you.

	statements 1–8	statements 9–16	statements 17–24	statements 25–32
TYPE	sanguine	melancholic	phlegmatic	choleric
My points				
Friend's evaluation				

....

Am I crazy?

WHAT IT'S ABOUT

It is the genesis of psychology: a trustworthy elderly man pushes a rectangular piece of blotting paper across his desk to you. On the paper is an inkblot. 'What could it be?' he asks you. For a long time, the famous Rorschach method was regarded as an 'X-ray of the soul', as a key to the subconscious. Messages from the subconscious were read into the patient's interpretations, which were then pseudo-scientifically analysed using algorithms.

THE TEST

The Rorschach method, named after the Swiss psychiatrist Hermann Rorschach, was based on a game named 'Klecksografie' or 'Blotto' that Rorschach loved to play as a child. You make an inkblot on a piece of paper, which you then fold down the middle so that when you open it up you have a completely symmetric image. Each player then describes what he or she can see: A butterfly? A giraffe with wings? Or perhaps even female genitalia? Rorschach, whose childhood friends called him 'Klecks' (Blot) because of

his obsession with the game, wanted to become an artist but ended up as a psychiatrist. He began to take a systematic approach to the game and turned it into an analytical method. According to Rorschach, when subjects were confronted with an ambiguous picture, it elicited free associations with their memories and suppressed emotions, enabling an interpretation of the subject's personality structure. While testing his method, he noticed that what schizophrenics saw in the inkblots was completely different from what non-schizophrenics saw. In 1921 he published the ten original ink pictures, which are still the ones used today.

The ten inkblot images – five coloured, five black-and-white – are shown to the subjects in a specific order. The psychiatrist categorises the answers using a complicated alphabetic code. Here are a few examples: 'W' stands for answers that apply to the blot as a whole, 'F' for answers that relate to the shape of the blot. 'M' stands for answers that contain a human movement, 'FM' for animal movements. Does a subject notice a person ('H'), an animal ('A') or only interpret the colour of the ink blot ('C')? A comprehensible answer is given a '+', an incomprehensible answer a '-', a conventional answer an 'o', an unusual one a 'u'. Popular answers are marked with a 'P'.

HOW IT'S EVALUATED

The trump card of projective tests – of which the Rorschach test is one – is also the joker. These are visual perception tests, in which the patient has more creative scope than in metric tests, which can result in helpful – and unexpected – answers. But by the same token, the psychiatrist's scope for interpretation is also greater, and therefore more questionable. Because different psychiatrists interpreted the same answer differently, the method fell into disrepute in the 1950s. In order to give it credibility again, the American psychologist John Ernest Exner began to compile norm values out of thousands of Rorschach protocols. Thanks to the 'Exner Scoring System' the test is approved in various countries including the USA, Brazil and Japan. In Europe, it is only occasionally used in forensics, and sometimes as a tool for personnel assessment, for example to find out how a job applicant reacts to an unusual or unexpected situation.

While attitudes to the inkblot test may differ widely, it will remain the third constant in the ancestral gallery of psychology next to Freud's couch and Pavlov's dog.

15

GOOD TO KNOW

You want to be 'average' when you do this test. Don't try to impress with creative answers. Genitals, blood and childhood memories will naturally awaken the psychiatrist's interest (which you don't want). If in doubt, say it as it is:
I see an inkblot.

The vast majority of people see a bat, a moth or a butterfly.

With the kind permission of the Hogrefe AG, Verlag Hans Huber

18

Who am I?

WHAT IT'S ABOUT

A little test to warm up with: Which five words would you use to describe yourself?

Over time, nearly every language has developed words to describe just about every personality trait: whatever you're like, however you feel, there will be a word to describe it. In the 1980s, the psychologists Paul Costa and Robert McCrae managed to prove that regardless of culture, every personality trait – no matter how unusual – belonged to one of the five following personality dimensions, the so-called 'Big Five':

1–Extraversion

Are you confident, active, cheerful, optimistic, sociable? Then you are extroverted. Low extraversion values are often erroneously interpreted as negative, although in fact they describe a person who is more independent than clingy, more balanced than insecure, more at peace with himself than concerned with getting approval from others. In short, can you manage to stand at a bar for five minutes without checking your phone (low value) or would you rather be dead than alone (high value)?

2–Agreeableness

Are you compassionate, sympathetic and empathetic towards others? Are you able to help others without thinking of how it could benefit you? Do you seek harmony or are you initially sceptical towards others? Are you quick to recognise mistakes and are you more competitive than cooperative? In short, do people like to work with you (high value) or do you rub people up the wrong way (low value)?

3–Conscientiousness

Do you consider yourself to be ambitious, persevering, systematic, fastidious to the point of being compulsive? Or would you describe yourself as laid-back to lethargic, calm verging on apathetic? In short, are you punctual (high value) or do you usually arrive late (low value)?

4–Emotional Stability (Neuroticism)

Are you laid-back and even-tempered, and do you recover

quickly from setbacks? Or are you always worrying and unsure and tend towards unrealistic ideas? In short, does your life consist of catastrophes that never happen (low value) or do conflicts roll off you like water off a duck's back (high value)?

5-Openness to experience

Are you curious, imaginative, and love to try out new things? Do you think outside the box and are you quick to change your mind? Or do you tend more towards conservative thinking and conventional solutions? In short, are you quickly bored (high value) or are you happiest when nothing rocks the boat (low value)?

The dominance of the Big Five in academic research can be explained with the 'lock-in' principle: Practically all psychological personality traits correlate with the five dimensions. The Big Five have become the standard, not because they are undisputed, but because they are the most commonly accepted reference values.

THE TEST

One of the most famous standard tests based on the Big Five approach is the NEO-PI-R. However, it consists of 240 questions and goes on forever. The psychologist Sam Gosling and his team have condensed the test to ten questions. Your TIPI (Ten-Item Personality Inventory) can be used as an initial approximation of the Big Five. Despite its brevity, the test on the following double page still gives a reliable result. Your result is compared to those of over 300,000 people, so that you can compare yourself to the norm.

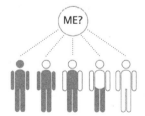

─────────── GOOD TO KNOW ───────────

When the personality test is used in the context of a job interview, most people judge themselves more positively than in a laboratory situation. But lying doesn't help – you're still the same person.

To what extent do the following descriptions apply to you on a scale of 1 (not at all) to 7 (absolutely)?

I see myself as

1. Extroverted, enthusiastic
2. Critical, quarrelsome
3. Dependable, self-disciplined
4. Anxious, easily upset
5. Open to new experiences, complex
6. Reserved, quiet
7. Sympathetic, warm
8. Disorganised, careless
9. Calm, emotionally stable
10. Conventional, uncreative

How to work out your score:

The items 2, 4, 6, 8 and 10 are inverted questions. Mirror the number that you entered: if you gave yourself a 1 then it becomes a 7. If you gave yourself a 7, it's a 1. A 6 is a 2 and vice versa. A 5 is a 3 and vice versa. A 4 stays a 4. After making these corrections, add up the values of the following pairs of questions and divide by 2.

1 and 6 = [ ] ÷ 2 = [ ] Extroversion

2 and 7 = [ ] ÷ 2 = [ ] Agreeableness

3 and 8 = [ ] ÷ 2 = [ ] Conscientiousness

4 and 9 = [ ] ÷ 2 = [ ] Emotional stability

5 and 10 = [ ] ÷ 2 = [ ] Openness to experience

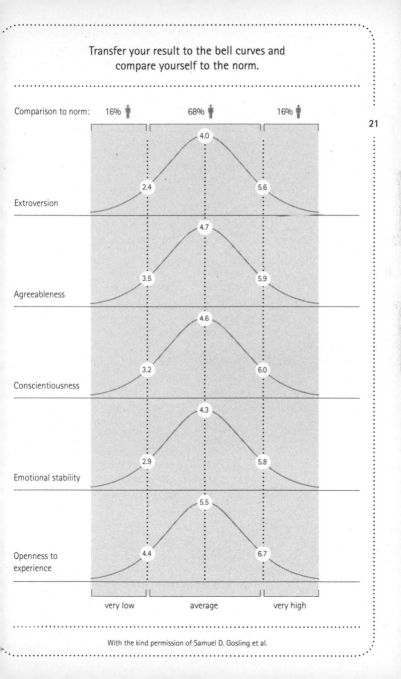

Transfer your result to the bell curves and
compare yourself to the norm.

Comparison to norm: 16%   68%   16%

4.0

Extroversion   2.4   5.6

4.7

Agreeableness   3.5   5.9

4.6

Conscientiousness   3.2   6.0

4.3

Emotional stability   2.9   5.8

5.5

Openness to experience   4.4   6.7

very low   average   very high

With the kind permission of Samuel D. Gosling et al.

Am I self-confident?

WHAT IT'S ABOUT

Self-confidence is the champagne of human emotions. Self-confident people are not better, more successful or better-looking than others, but they are happier. They don't make less wrong decisions than others, but they suffer less for them. They, too, feel anger, sorrow and despair, but without losing their self-respect.

Unlike the excessive self-love of narcissists (→ Narcissism Test, p. 26), somebody with real self-confidence feels good about themselves regardless of what others might think or say. If we don't care what other people think of us, we are self-confident. Psychologists don't talk about self-confidence but about self-esteem. According to the psychologist Nathaniel Branden, there are six pillars of self-esteem. We like ourselves when we:

1 – live and act consciously. When we don't suppress anything.
2 – accept ourselves the way we are.
3 – have control over our own lives.
4 – don't feel the need to please others, but stay true to our convictions.
5 – have a goal in life.
6 – live authentically, i.e. when our thoughts, actions and feelings are more or less in harmony.

Question: Can a condition like this be measured?

THE TEST

The most famous self-confidence test is the 'Rosenberg Self-Esteem Scale' from 1965. Since then, hundreds of other scales and tests have addressed this theme, one of the most interesting of which is the 'Core Self-Evaluation Scale' (CSES) developed by Timothy A. Judge and his team in 2002. The test is designed not only to assess our self-esteem, but three other areas too: Firstly, our self-efficacy, i.e. how well we perform across a variety of situations. Secondly, our neuroticism, i.e. how badly we react to stress and are susceptible to feelings of helplessness. Thirdly, our locus of control, i.e. how strongly we believe that we are in charge of our own destiny. By answering the

12 questions, you end up with a CSE value of between 1 and 5.

HOW IT'S EVALUATED

A high CSE value basically means you have high self-esteem. A low value indicates self-doubt. Comparative studies have shown that those with a high score are usually also happier in their jobs. Those with a low score are usually unhappy in their jobs. People with a good work-life balance (→ Stress Test, p. 118), have a higher CSE value. However, no correlations were found between high self-esteem and success. Note: a characteristic of successful people is that they are not self-confident and suffer from self-doubt. So you shouldn't worry if you get a 'bad' score. Even worse than having weaknesses is not knowing your weaknesses.

GOOD TO KNOW

'If one only wished to be happy, this could be easily accomplished; but we wish to be happier than other people, and this is always difficult, for we believe others to be happier than they are.' *Montesquieu*

To what extent do the following statements apply to you?

completely untrue 1 — 2 — 3 — 4 — 5 completely true

1. I am confident that I get the success I deserve in life.

   1 — 2 — 3 — 4 — 5

2. Sometimes I feel depressed.

   1 — 2 — 3 — 4 — 5

3. When I try, I generally succeed.

   1 — 2 — 3 — 4 — 5

4. Sometimes when I fail I feel worthless.

   1 — 2 — 3 — 4 — 5

5. I complete tasks successfully.

   1 — 2 — 3 — 4 — 5

6. Sometimes I do not feel in control of my work.

   1 — 2 — 3 — 4 — 5

7. Overall, I am satisfied with myself.

   1 — 2 — 3 — 4 — 5

8. I am filled with doubts about my competence.

(1) — 2 — 3 — 4 — 5

9. I determine what will happen in my life.

1 — 2 — 3 — 4 — (5)

10. I don't feel in control of my career success.

(1) — 2 — 3 — 4 — 5

11. I am capable of coping with most of my problems.

1 — 2 — 3 — 4 — (5)

12. There are times when things look pretty bleak and hopeless for me.

(1) — 2 — 3 — 4 — 5

. . . .

Add up your points.

⚠ The statements 2, 4, 6, 8, 10 and 12 are reverse scored. That means 1 is a 5 and vice versa, a 2 is a 4 and vice versa, and a 3 remains a 3. To work out your CSE value, divide your total number of points by 12:

58

< 3 = low CSE value   3–4 = average CSE value   > 4 = high CSE value

. . . .

For orientation purposes only. You can find links to standardised values in the Sources.

26

How narcissistic am I?

WHAT IT'S ABOUT

The word narcissism comes from the Greek legend of the beautiful Narcissus (type: Cristiano Ronaldo), who gave the nymph Echo the cold shoulder. The avenging goddess Nemesis punished his arrogance by making him fall in love with the reflection of his own beautiful face in a pool. Finding that his love could not be requited, Narcissus pined away and died. Narcissists are people who need to be admired and at the same time are afraid of being slighted, who come across as self-confident but feel threatened in relationships as soon as they do not meet with approval. Above all, narcissists have fragile self-esteem, and are unable to relate to others. The egomania of 'covert narcissists', on the other hand, reveals itself not in cockiness but in vulnerability. They react hyper-sensitively to criticism, are quick to feel belittled, but at the same time are constantly watching and judging others.

THE TEST

The Narcissism questionnaire by Henry Murray from 1938 was updated in 2013 by a team of psychologists led by Jonathan Cheek (Maladaptive Covert Narcissism Scale, MCNS), to make it easier to identify covert narcissists.

HOW IT'S EVALUATED

Don't be shocked if you get a high score in this test. Many studies suggest that we are living in a 'narcissistic age'. Since 1979 the University of Michigan has been using the 'Interpersonal Reactivity Index' to measure students' level of empathy. Results show that students today are 40 per cent less empathetic than they were 20 years ago. Another study found out that narcissism levels are rising. Life is becoming more superficial and self-interest comes above all.

GOOD TO KNOW

A quick test, developed at the University of Berkeley: Ask six people to sit at a round table and have a conversation. The next day, ask each person where they sat at the table. Narcissists are more likely to answer: At the head of the table.

Evaluate yourself.

does not apply at all ① — 2 — 3 — 4 — ⑤ applies strongly

1. I can become completely absorbed in thinking about my personal affairs, my health or my relationship to others.

   ① — 2 — 3 — 4 — 5

2. My feelings are easily hurt by the slighting remarks of others.

   ① — 2 — 3 — 4 — 5

3. When I enter a room I often become self-conscious and feel like everyone is looking at me.

   ① — 2 — 3 — 4 — 5

4. I don't like sharing the credit of achievement with others.

   ① — 2 — 3 — 4 — 5

5. I feel that I have enough on my hands without worrying about other people's problems.

   ① — 2 — 3 — 4 — 5

6. I feel that I am different from most people.

   ① — 2 — ✗ — 4 — 5

7. I often interpret the critical remarks of others in a personal way.

   ① — 2 — 3 — 4 — 5

8. I easily become wrapped up in my own interests and forget the existence of others.

1 — 2 — 3 — 4 — 5

9. I dislike being with a group unless I know that I am appreciated by at least one of those present.

1 — 2 — 3 — 4 — 5

10. I am secretly annoyed when other people come to me with their troubles, and ask for sympathy.

1 — 2 — 3 — 4 — 5

11. I am jealous of good-looking people.

1 — 2 — 3 — 4 — 5

12. I tend to feel humiliated when criticised.

1 — 2 — 3 — 4 — 5

13. I wonder why other people aren't more appreciative of my talents and good qualities.

1 — 2 — 3 — 4 — 5

14. I see other people as being either great or terrible.

1 — 2 — 3 — 4 — 5

15. I sometimes have fantasies about being violent without knowing why.

1 — 2 — 3 — 4 — 5

16. I am especially sensitive to success and failure.

1 — 2 — 3 — 4 — 5

17. Other people don't seem to understand my problems.

1 — 2 — 3 — 4 — 5

18. I try to avoid rejection at all costs.

1 — 2 — 3 — 4 — 5

19. I think my secret thoughts, feelings and actions would horrify some of my friends.

1 — 2 — 3 — 4 — 5

20. I tend to become involved in relationships in which I alternately adore and despise the other person.

1 — 2 — 3 — 4 — 5

21. Even when I am in a group of friends, I often feel alone and uneasy.

1 — 2 — 3 — 4 — 5

22. I resent others who have what I lack.

1 — 2 — 3 — 4 — 5

23. Defeat or disappointment usually shame or anger me, but I try not to show it.

1 — 2 — 3 — 4 — 5

....

Add up your points:

< 50 = low level of covert narcissism
50 – 80 = medium level of covert narcissism
> 80 = high level of covert narcissism

....

With the kind permission of Jonathan Cheek, Wellesley College

Who is lying to me?

WHAT IT'S ABOUT

Fear is the essence of lying. Somebody who lies is afraid of being found out, so if you suspect someone of lying you have to watch out for signs of fear. But what are these signs?

THE TEST

It is important not to forget the basic rule that you don't *hear* a lie, you see it. The liar blushes, brushes his hand over his face, or crosses his arms. He diverts his gaze or seeks eye contact to check if the other person has fallen for his lie. A thousand years ago in ancient China, suspects were made to do the rice test, as a dry mouth was thought to be a sign that you were lying. The suspect was given rice grains that he had to keep in his mouth and then spit out after the interview. If the rice was dry he was a liar. In principle, a polygraph – or lie-detector – works in a similar way, by recording pulse, blood pressure, breathing and electrodermal activity, i.e. sweating caused by stress. The test consists of three types of question:

1 – **Irrelevant questions:** 'Were you born in Manchester?' The interrogators get an idea of how the suspect behaves when he tells the truth.

2 – **Control questions not relevant to the event:** 'Have you ever been to a brothel?' The interviewers see how the suspect reacts to stress.

3 – **Relevant questions about the event:** 'Where were you yesterday at 11 p.m.?'

HOW IT'S EVALUATED

The suspect's stress reactions to the control questions are compared to his reactions to the event questions. However, the method is controversial because the interrogation situation in itself causes as much stress as being confronted with a lie.

--------- GOOD TO KNOW ---------

How to get through a lie detector test: Breathe normally but quickly; try to identify the three types of question being asked. Answer the control questions either holding your breath or breathing quickly in order to confuse the test. If your stress reactions to the control questions are stronger than to the relevant ones, the test loses its validity.

The Nine Steps of Interrogation

The Reid® Technique consists of three phases: the Fact Analysis, followed by the Behaviour Analysis Interview (which is a non-confrontational interview designed to develop investigative and behavioural information), followed by, when appropriate, the Reid Nine Steps of Interrogation. Interrogation is only appropriate if the investigative information indicates that the subject is withholding relevant information.

1 – The positive confrontation
Begin by advising the suspect that the investigation suggests he is not telling the truth. Then change from a dominating and accusatory tone to one of understanding.

2 – Theme development
Obtaining an admission of guilt is easier if the suspect is given the opportunity to give a reason or excuse that allows him to preserve some of his self-respect. Help him to develop 'themes' or reasons that enable him to justify the crime ('The bank isn't exactly squeaky clean either.')

3 – Handling denials
Don't let him verbalise his denials. The more often he says 'It wasn't me!' the stronger his resistance becomes, and the harder it is to get a confession out of him.

4 – Overcoming objections
Give the suspect the opportunity to explain why he could not possibly have committed the crime ('I've got enough money!'). Then discuss, hypothetically, why he might have committed it.

5 – Procuring and retaining the suspect's attention
Any suspect who is going to confess moves from an offensive to a defensive mode. At this point you should move physically closer to the suspect.

6 – Handling the suspect's passive mood
Now you have to focus on signs that suggest the suspect is giving up (tears, for example).

7 – Presenting an alternative question
Offer the suspect two possible choices as to how the crime was committed, one of which is less incriminating.

8 – Detailing the offence
If he confesses, search for details. Ask questions that only the perpetrator can answer.

9 – Oral and written statements
The oral statement must be recorded in writing and signed. Include errors in the report. If the suspect corrects them, it shows the court that he knew what he was signing.

32

What does my handwriting reveal about me?

THE SUBJECT

Every person's handwriting is unique, which is why for a long time it was considered the 'facsimile of the brain'. By analysing a person's handwriting, it was thought that you could infer his or her character and abilities. The founder of modern graphology was Jean-Hippolyte Michon, who gave the discipline its name in his work *Système de Graphologie*. In the 1930s Max Pulver linked graphology to psychoanalysis and provided a means of working out the symbolic value of handwriting.

THE TEST

A graphological analysis is not a test in the sense of a standardised process, but a technique that looks at stroke structure, handwriting style and the spacing on the page. The speed of writing, size of letters, pressure of the pen, the level of embellishment, the slant, and the size of the gaps between letters also play a role. The evaluator analyses an A4 page of writing and deduces highly specific characteristics of the test person, such as motivational ability, loyalty, diligence, and frustration tolerance.

THE EVALUATION

From the 1960s on, handwriting analysis was regarded as a reliable instrument for evaluating a prospective employee. But with the onward march of digitalisation, handwriting is all but disappearing – and with it, graphology's means of evaluation.

On the right you can see how the graphologist Markus Furrer assessed Roman Tschäppeler, the co-author of this book.

GOOD TO KNOW

Handwriting may be dying out, but computer writing also reveals something about us: the rhythm and speed with which we type frequently used words, such as passwords, is unique. Keystroke recognition is the technical term for this form of identification.

This is my best handwriting.
Is it legible? What does
the graphologist say?

The degree of tension in the handwriting reveals whether our energies flow in a self-assured and therefore relaxed manner, or in a hesitant and therefore inhibited manner. The movement of the writer's hand is more tense than relaxed, but by no means overly strained or cramped. This means there is tautness in the flow of his energies. He is engaged, ambitious and challenges himself. He is not overly calm or relaxed, but also not overly highly strung, so he is able to relax.

The shape of the letters indicates the writer's type of personality. Our writer shapes his letters clearly, comprehensibly, simply, unpretentiously, without any posing or affectation. That means he has his own style – independent and comprehensible to others. He is somebody who doesn't present a mask to the outside world, who is authentic and focused on what's important. He takes a clear stance on things, when necessary critically and assertively, but not idiosyncratically, because his 'shape' is respectful of conventions.

Brief analysis by Markus Furrer, lic. phil. psychologist (SBAP) specialising in handwriting, graphologist (SGG)

34

How emotionally intelligent am I?

WHAT IT'S ABOUT

In 1930, American psychologist Edward Lee Thorndike made an interesting observation: popular people are not those who are brilliant themselves, but those who make us feel brilliant. We like to be around people who make us better than we really are. Thorndike regarded the skill of letting others shine as a form of intelligence – 'social intelligence'. It took over 60 years until the American journalist Daniel Goleman popularised the idea in his bestseller *EQ*. He drew on the research of the two social psychologists John D. Mayer and Peter Salovey, whose findings he categorised into four 'domains':

1 – Self-awareness: Do you interpret your emotions properly? Do you know why you feel happy or unhappy?
2 – Self management: Are you able to control your emotions?
3 – Empathy: Can you recognise how others are feeling?
4 – Relationship management: Are you able to influence other people's emotions and moods?

THE TEST

The MSCEIT™ (Mayer-Salovey-Caruso Emotional Intelligence Test) is used to ascertain emotional intelligence. Its EQ scale ranges from 55 to 145, with values over 115 considered above-average. Emotional Intelligence is particularly useful for modern personnel management. Inspiring instead of intimidating, admitting to your mistakes, promoting team work and collaboration, and encouraging participation – these are the skills required by the next generation of managers.

The MSCEIT™ is very comprehensive, and filling it out takes around half an hour. Our method reduces the EQ to one single question.

GOOD TO KNOW

If you feel good in the presence of someone, chances are high, s/he is emotionally intelligent.

The one-question EQ test:

....

What sport do I do?

....

Have you chosen a team sport or an individual sporting discipline?

A phenomenon that has received a lot of attention in Norway is that top managers prefer individual sporting disciplines. In particular, they like to 'relax' outside work doing extreme sports in which they alone are responsible for achieving their goal. On the whole, these managers are also very high performers at work and surpass their objectives, but their social skills are weak (→ The Leadership Test, p. 106). In other words, their emotional intelligence is not very developed.

....

36

How do I handle money?

WHAT IT'S ABOUT

When psychologists research the subject of risk, their favourite barometer is money. Nothing says more about a person's predisposition to risk than their willingness to gamble with their own income.

THE TEST

Imagine you need a new pair of trainers. You have to decide whether to buy the same pair as last time (a style that you were satisfied with), or another style. There is no difference in price, and the other advantages and disadvantages of the two seem to balance each other out. How do you decide?

If you choose the new trainers, you are a risk taker. You choose the option that has a higher chance of winning and a higher chance of losing, because the shoes could surpass your expectations or you might be disappointed. If you choose the old style, you are more afraid of risk. You don't want to risk making a loss and are therefore willing to miss out on a potential gain. Of course, this example is harmless. But what if it's an investment or a

pension that's at stake, and not a pair of trainers?

Even those who can't tell a stock from a bond know that investing money is problematic. Ideally we want a secure, risk-free investment that is also profitable. But it is almost impossible to make a profit without taking a risk.

You could just ask yourself how willing you are to take risks. However, from the point of view of behavioural psychology, it is more interesting to ask how 'risk tolerant' you are. Because it is not really about how much you like to take risks (whether you like skydiving or drove your parents' car when you were a teenager), but how well you can deal with the prospect of making a loss. Because when it comes to decision-making, losing has a greater psychological impact than winning. There are four different aspects of risk tolerance:

1 – **Risk ability or risk acceptance:** Which loss can you cope with?

2 – **Willingness to take a risk:** Which loss are you willing to take?

3 – **Necessity of risk:** What level of risk do you need to take in order to

achieve your objectives?
4 – Ability to carry a risk: How long can you, and how long do you want to carry the burden of particular risk?

HOW IT'S EVALUATED

The Swiss economist Petra Jörg Perrin carried out a meta-study in which she analysed various factors that influence risk tolerance. Unsurprisingly, the extent of a person's financial assets played a decisive role: a person with a lot of money is more willing to take risks than someone who can't afford to lose much without losing everything. Freelancers are bigger risk-takers than employees. Men are bigger risk-takers than women. The study also found that the more educated people are, the more willing they are to take risks. Marriage, children and a mortgage reduce risk tolerance, presumably because you are also responsible for others and not just yourself. Religious people are also less willing to take risks. Ethnicity, on the other hand, does not play a role. And finally, people who smoke, drink and are underinsured are bigger risk-takers.

———————— GOOD TO KNOW ————————

Before making a decision, weigh up the probability of an undesired event coming to pass against the negative consequence if it does come to pass.

Place a cross next to the answer that applies to you and calculate your risk tolerance.

....

1. How long can you manage without the money that you want to invest? Don't forget to calculate big purchases and losses (renovations, sabbatical, children, etc.)

   (0) < 2 years   (2) 6–10 years
   (1) 2–5 years   (3) >10 years

2. If you take away the planned amount that you want to invest, how much money do you have available in case of an emergency?

   (0) 1 month's salary   (2) 7-12 months' salary
   (1) 2-6 months' salary   (3) 1 year's salary

3. How much of your current annual salary could you save?

   (0) Nothing   (2) About 2 month's salary
   (1) About one month's salary   (3) > 2 month's salary

4. Presuming you could invest £20,000: what strategy would you choose?

   (0) After 5 years you have a 50/50 chance of having 20,000 or 22,000
   (1) After 5 years you have a 50/50 chance of having 19,000 or 23,000
   (2) After 5 years you have a 50/50 chance of having 18,000 or 24,000
   (3) After 5 years you have a 50/50 chance of having 12,000 or 30,000

5. Depending on the planned length of investment, how do you think the economy will develop during that time?

   (0) No idea   (2) Neutral (stagnation)
   (1) Negative (recession)   (3) Positive (growth)

6. Presuming you would invest a significant amount in stocks and shares, how would you react if their value dropped by over 30 per cent in a short period of time?

   (0) Sell them all immediately   (2) Wait
   (1) Sell some of the shares   (3) Buy more

1. Add up your points for questions 1–3
   (the values are next to the check box). Insert the total on the vertical axis 'Ability to take risks'.

2. Add up the points for questions 4–6.
   Insert the total on the horizontal axis 'Willingness to take risks'.

3. Read the results.

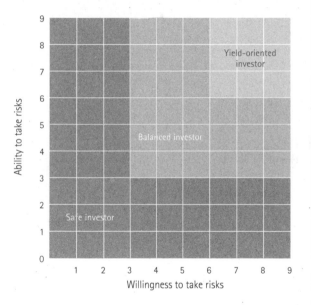

40

Am I generous?

WHAT IT'S ABOUT

According to the 'Rational Choice Theory' all of our actions are motivated by self-interest. The theory converges with the model of the 'Homo oeconomicus', whose actions are geared only towards profit maximisation. However, a series of tests indicate that humans also behave differently and, in part, selflessly.

THE TEST

A test person is confronted with eight alternatives of how to divide up money between himself and an unknown person. Somebody who keeps 100 dollars and gives the other person 50 dollars is 'individualistic'. Somebody who divides it up so that each person gets 75 dollars is 'prosocial' – at least according to the Social Value Orientation Scale developed by the psychologists Don Griesinger and Jim Livingston in 1973, which differentiates between eight different orientations.

THE EVALUATION

Competitive: You regard the other person's loss as your gain. You think: win-lose.

Individualistic: You are primarily interested in your own profit, less in the loss of the other person. You think: win.

Prosocial: Your goal is for everybody to profit from your decision. You think: win-win.

Altruistic: You want to help others. You think lose-win and experience this as a personal satisfaction.

These four 'common' orientations have four pathological counterparts: Sadism (extreme competitiveness, whereby you enjoy it when other people lose), sadomasochism (your goal is that neither you nor the other person wins), masochism (you want to lose), and martyrdom (you lose, so that others win).

─── GOOD TO KNOW ───

'Giving a gift means giving another person something that you would actually like to keep for yourself.' *Selma Lagerlöf*

Select which way you would divide up the money and mark with a cross.
Then find out where you stand in the model below.

	A	B	C	D	E	F	G	H
	☐	☐	☐	☐	☐	☐	☐	☐
Money for me $	50	85	100	85	50	15	0	15
Money for others $	100	85	50	15	0	15	50	85

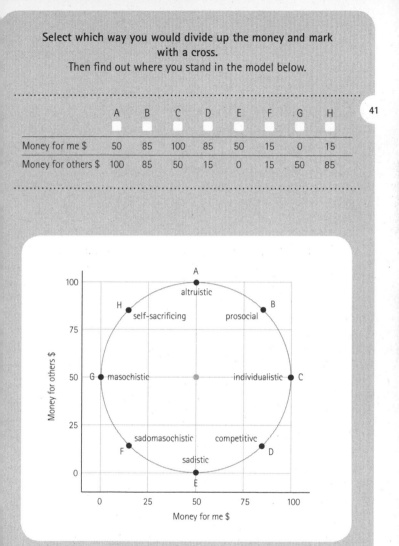

This is only an approximation of your actual profile. The researchers Ryan O. Murphy and his colleagues at ETH Zurich offer a great test on their website http://vlab.ethz.ch (SVO Slider Measure), which gives you a more precise result.

What type am I?

WHAT IT'S ABOUT

When Katharine Briggs, a housewife from Washington DC, first met her future son-in-law, she was a little sceptical about her daughter's choice. She was fascinated by his practical, detail-oriented personality that was so different from her own more intuitive character. In order to find out if he was the right man for her daughter, she developed a questionnaire based on the 'psychological types' defined by the psychoanalyst C. G. Jung. A few years later, in 1941, she presented the Myers-Briggs Type Indicator, MBTI® for short, which she developed together with her daughter Isabel Briggs Myers. This mother of all personality tests is today one of the most well-known methods for assessing personality types, and is particularly popular in the USA. Most of the *Fortune 500* companies use it, and 1.5 million Americans do the test every year. It is also known that McKinsey management consultants are able to recite their personal code ('ENTJ', 'ISFP') off by heart like their own phone number. The codes are put on display before the start of a project, so that everyone knows whom they will be dealing with.

THE TEST

The actual test is a questionnaire. Fifty questions elicit 16 personality types, each of which has a four-letter code. Rule of thumb: All types are positive, you cannot perform badly or fail. The test is made up of four pairs of opposites:

Extrovert (E) and introvert (I): How you are energised

Extroverts draw their energy from interacting with others, introverts from thinking about ideas and concepts alone.

Sensing (S) and intuition (N): How you perceive and take in information

People who veer towards sensing believe in facts and details. Intuitive people look for connections and believe in future possibilities.

Thinking (T) and feeling (F): How you process information

Thinkers make decisions based on analysing the facts. Feeling people do whatever is necessary to establish harmony.

Judgement (J) and perception (P): How you orient yourself to the outside world

Judgers are organised, tidy and methodical. Perceivers are spontaneous, flexible, and keep all options open for as long as possible.

☛ Make a spontaneous assessment of yourself. Are you more extroverted (E) or introverted (I)? Do you focus on facts (S) or are you intuitive (N)? Are you more rational (T) or emotional (F)? Are you a planner (J) or do you like to remain flexible (P)? What is your code? Read the precise type descriptions on the next two double pages.

HOW IT'S EVALUATED

The test does not measure disposition, abilities or character; instead it identifies your personality 'preferences' based on the four pairs of opposite personality types. Your four-letter code is made up of the letters that you choose from each pair. But why is it important if you're an 'ENTP' or an 'INTJ'? Because we can only understand others when we know ourselves. That may sound

like psychobabble, but is in fact very important when we work together with other people. If we can't understand and accept that others work or think differently from us, we will never be able to complete a project successfully together. It doesn't matter if the type description doesn't fit you exactly, it's more about gaining awareness that people have very different ways of working. A few examples: A person who likes to make decisions based on data (S) may come across as detail-focused and pedantic to a person who is interested in the big picture and makes decisions intuitively (N). People who are extrovert (E) often have difficulties understanding introverted people (I); they think they are shy or misinterpret their reticence as arrogance or incompetence. Introverts, on the other hand, see extroverts as superficial, erratic and overly talkative. A 'J', who will organise a job with the deadline clearly in mind, will be driven mad by a 'P', who tends to keep all options open to the last minute. But if they know, with the help of the letter codes, how the other person ticks, they will be more trusting and tolerant of the person's behaviour.

GOOD TO KNOW

However sceptical you may be of any kind of personality test, there is one thing that is helpful to know and which is good to keep in mind the next time you are working in a group. People find their energy in two different ways: either in a group (E) or when they are alone (I). Knowing this can make everything much simpler.

Here are the 16 different MBTI® types.

Ask yourself what type you are. Or ask someone who knows you well to categorise you.

☐ ISTJ

You are quiet and serious, and earn success through thoroughness and dependability. You are practical, matter-of-fact, realistic, and responsible. You decide logically what should be done and work towards it steadily, regardless of distractions. You take pleasure in making everything orderly and organised – your work, your home, your life. You value traditions and loyalty.

☐ INFJ

You seek meaning and connection in ideas, relationships, and material possessions. You want to understand what motivates people and are insightful about others. You are conscientious and committed to your firm values. You have a clear vision about how best to serve the common good and are organised and decisive in implementing this vision.

☐ ISFJ

You are quiet, friendly, responsible and conscientious. You are committed and steady in meeting your obligations, and are thorough and painstaking, verging on fastidious. You are loyal and considerate, and notice and remember specifics about people who are important to you. You strive to create an orderly and harmonious environment at work and at home.

☐ INTJ

You have an original mind and great drive for implementing your ideas and achieving your goals. You quickly see patterns in external events and develop long-range explanatory perspectives. When you are motivated, you are well-organised and reliable. You are sceptical and independent, have high standards of competence and performance – for yourself and others.

☐ ISTP

You are tolerant and flexible, and a quiet observer until a problem appears, then you act quickly to find workable solutions. You analyse what makes things work and readily get through large amounts of data to get to the root of a problem. You are interested in cause and effect, organise facts using logical principles and value efficiency.

☐ INFP

You are idealistic, loyal to your values and to people who are important to you. You want to live your life according to your values. You are curious, quick to see possibilities, and implement ideas. You want to understand people and to help them fulfil their potential. You are adaptable, flexible and accepting unless your values are threatened.

☐ ISFP

You are quiet, friendly, sensitive and kind. You are able to enjoy the present moment, and like to have your own space and to work within your own time frame. You are loyal and committed to your values and to people who are important to you. You dislike disagreements and conflicts, and would never force your opinions or values on others.

☐ INTP

You seek to develop logical explanations for everything that interests you. You are theoretical and abstract and interested more in ideas than in social interaction. You are quiet, contained, flexible and adaptable. You have an unusual ability to focus in depth to solve problems. You are sceptical, sometimes critical and always analytical.

☐ ESTP

You are flexible and tolerant and take a pragmatic approach focused on immediate results. You are bored by theories and conceptual explanations, you want to act energetically to solve a problem. You focus on the here and now, are spontaneous, and enjoy doing things with others. You enjoy material comforts and style. You learn best through doing.

☐ ENFP

You are enthusiastic and imaginative and see life as full of possibilities. You make connections between events and information very quickly, and confidently proceed based on the patterns you see. You want a lot of affirmation from others, and readily give appreciation and support. You are spontaneous and flexible, often rely on your ability to improvise and on your verbal fluency.

☐ ESFP

You are outgoing, friendly and accepting. You love life, people and material comforts. You enjoy working with others and making things happen. You bring common sense and a realistic approach to your work, and make work fun. You are flexible and spontaneous, and adapt readily to new people and environments. You learn best by trying a new skill with other people.

☐ ENTP

You are quick, ingenious, stimulating, alert and outspoken. You are resourceful in solving new and challenging problems. You are adept at generating conceptual possibilities and analysing them strategically. You are good at reading other people. You are bored by routine, will seldom do the same thing the same way, and are apt to turn your interest to one new thing after another.

☐ ESTJ

You are practical, realistic and matter-of-fact. You are decisive, and quick to implement decisions. You organise projects and people to get things done and focus on getting results in the most efficient way possible. You take care of routine details. You have a clear set of logical standards that you systematically follow – and you expect the same of others.

☐ ENFJ

You are warm, empathetic, responsive and responsible. You are highly attuned to the emotions, needs and motivations of others. You see potential in everyone and want to help others fulfil their potential. You may act as a catalyst for individual and group growth. You are loyal and responsive to praise and criticism. You are sociable, facilitate others in a group and provide inspiring leadership.

☐ ESFJ

You are warm-hearted, conscientious and cooperative. You want harmony in your environment, and work with determination to establish it. You like to work with others to complete tasks accurately and on time. You are loyal and follow through even in small matters. You notice what others need in their day-to-day lives and try to provide it. You want to be appreciated for what you are and for what you contribute.

☐ ENTJ

You are frank, decisive, and assume leadership readily. You are quick to recognise illogical and inefficient procedures and policies, and develop and implement comprehensive systems to solve organisational problems. You enjoy long-term planning and goal setting. You are usually well informed, well read, enjoy expanding your knowledge and passing it on to others. You are forceful in presenting your ideas.

Body
& health

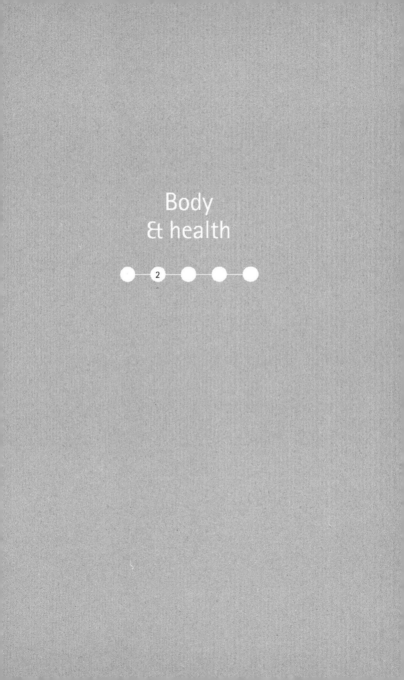

Do I drink too much?

WHAT IT'S ABOUT

The crucial question for a drinker is: How much is too much? From a sober perspective, the rule of thumb is 'If you need it, then you're addicted'. If you want to be a bit more lenient, you could ask: 'From what time in the day is it OK to consume alcohol?' i.e. what time is it OK to head down to the pub after work. Of course, the great thing about after-work drinking is that you drink on an empty stomach, which is a ticket to both heaven and hell: Heaven, because there is no sweeter form of intoxication than one that begins with a quickly downed pint and ends after three. Hell, because alcohol is a friend that always takes more than it gives.

THE TEST

Doctors distinguish between abstinence, unproblematic consumption, problematic consumption and addiction. To quickly diagnose whether a patient is heading from problematic consumption towards addiction, they use the CAGE test:

1 – Have you ever thought that you should drink less? (C as in Cut down on drinking)
2 – Have you ever got annoyed at other people for criticising your drinking habits? (A for Annoyance)
3 – Have you ever felt guilty about the amount of alcohol you consume? (G for Guilty)
4 – Have you ever needed to drink alcohol in the morning to feel on top of things? (E for Eye-opener)

HOW IT'S EVALUATED

If you answered two of the four questions with a Yes, there is a high chance that you are addicted, and it would be advisable to undergo further clinical-psychological screenings. But if even if you're not addicted, you might still have problematic consumption. To find out if this is the case, do the test on the right page.

GOOD TO KNOW

'Alcohol preserves everything – except dignity and secrets.' *Robert Lembke*

Make a cross next to the answer that applies to you.

The AUDIT-C questionnaire from the WHO tests whether your alcohol consumption is problematic.

☛ 1 unit of drink = ½ pint of beer, 1 small glass of wine, 1 single measure of spirits

1. How often do you have a drink containing alcohol?
    - A Never
    - B Once a month or less
    - C 2–4 times a month
    - D 2–4 times a week
    - E 4 times or more a week

2. How many units of alcohol do you drink on a typical day when you are drinking?
    - A 1–2 units
    - B 3–4 units
    - C 5–6 units
    - D 7–9 units
    - E 10+ units

3. How often do you drink 6 or more units on a single occasion?
    - A Never
    - B Less than once a month
    - C Once a month
    - D Once a week
    - E Daily or nearly daily

Add up all the points you crossed: A = 0 B = 1 C = 2 D = 3 E = 4

A total of 5+ is 'Audit-C positive', i.e. indicates problematic consumption.

☛ This test is not a substitute for an expert diagnosis

With the kind permission of WHO, Department of Mental Health and Substance Dependence, Geneva. AUDIT, the Alcohol Use Disorders Identification Test (2001)

52

Am I depressed?

THE SUBJECT

Without Sigmund Freud, the couch would just be a normal piece of furniture. But what is normal, anyway? And am I normal? To find out if a patient is just going through a difficult patch or is actually suffering from depression, it is sometimes enough to ask just two questions.

THE TEST

'Two questions are as good as many' is the title of a ground-breaking article by American psychologists, who in 1996 observed that you could tell if a patient was suffering from depression simply from his or her answers to two questions.

THE EVALUATION

Of course, questionnaires and rapid tests generally only provide indications, never proof, of a psychological problem. A valid medical diagnosis of depression can only be made by a trained psychologist using a standardised patient interview. Indeed, (self) tests in the area of clinical psychology are still a long way from replacing the experience and expertise of a human doctor.

The idea for the two-question test arose from the observation that it is usually GPs who are the first to be confronted with their patients' depression symptoms. Many doctors found conventional questionnaires too detailed and time-consuming. This led to the development of the two-question depression test, which proved to be a useful shortcut for finding out whether the patient should be referred to a psychologist.

Besides the two-question test, there are many other patient self-analysis questionnaires (Patient Health Questionnaires, PHQ): phqscreeners.com

---

GOOD TO KNOW

'Happy is he who forgets what he cannot change.' *Karl Haffner*

The two questions

....

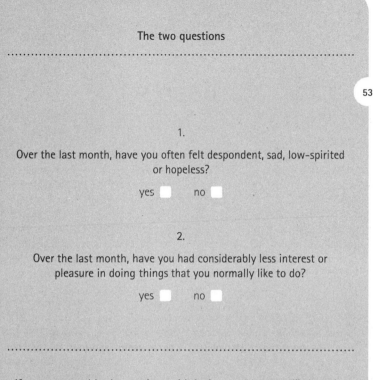

1.

Over the last month, have you often felt despondent, sad, low-spirited or hopeless?

yes ☐   no ☐

2.

Over the last month, have you had considerably less interest or pleasure in doing things that you normally like to do?

yes ☐   no ☐

....

If you answered both questions with 'no', you are very unlikely to be suffering from depression. If you answered 'yes' once and 'no' once, you should watch out for other typical symptoms such as insomnia, restlessness, feelings of guilt, concentration problems, lack of motivation and suicidal tendencies. If you answered both questions with 'yes', you should seek expert medical advice.

....

PHQ-2 is the ultra-short form of the PHQ-D. Developed by R. L. Spitzer, J. B. Williams and K. Kroenke.

Am I too fat?

WHAT IT'S ABOUT

We all know the dangers of obesity, and what we could or should do about it: No carbohydrates after 6 pm! No sugar! Walk 10,000 steps a day! But when do you weigh too much and when do you need to start taking action?

THE TEST

For a long time the benchmark was the Body-Mass Index, or BMI for short. In 1997 it was adopted as a standard by the WHO, and its success is due not least to the fact that it is easy to calculate (weight divided by height squared) and provides clear results: underweight (>18.5), normal (18.5–24.9), over-weight (25–29.9), obese (>30).

HOW IT'S EVALUATED

But the index has its weaknesses. Firstly, the overweight boundary of 25 was made rather arbitrarily (when the Public Health Service in the USA adopted the threshold value in 1998, 35 million American were suddenly overweight). Secondly, the BMI does not take into account physique, body fat percentage, sex or age. The test only becomes convincing if you compare different body values.

The **Waist-to-Height Ratio (WHtR)** is defined as a person's waist circumference divided by the person's height, and measures body fat distribution around the waist area. **Skin fold measurements** on the stomach, triceps and hips for women, and the stomach, chest and thighs for men, is the most accurate way of testing fat distribution in the body. The **bioelectrical impedance analysis** measures body compo-sition (fat and muscle mass and body water) by means of an electric current through the body tissues. Muscles are heavier than fat. A high BMI with a high percentage of muscles is not as bad as a high BMI with a high percentage of fat.

GOOD TO KNOW

'Making the weight' or 'boiling down' is how boxers describe their quick weight loss before a fight. Drink little, do exercise in non-breathable rain gear (so that you sweat more) and take diuretics. This method is not to be recommended.

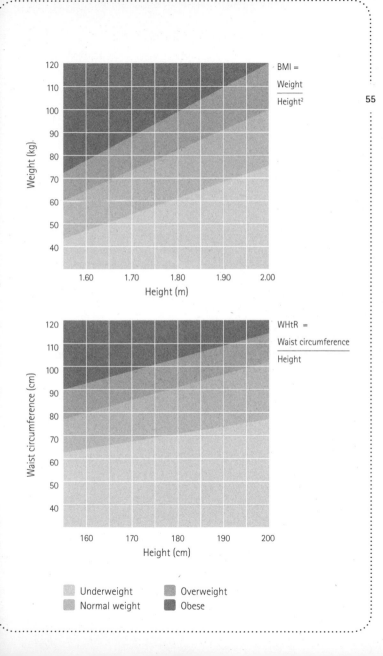

BMI = $\dfrac{\text{Weight}}{\text{Height}^2}$

WHtR = $\dfrac{\text{Waist circumference}}{\text{Height}}$

Underweight   Overweight

Normal weight   Obese

How strong am I?

WHAT IT'S ABOUT

The push-up is one of the oldest exercise techniques and still feared as much as it is loved. It probably originates from yoga – the sixth position of the sun salutation sequence, the Chaturanga Dandasana, is similar to a traditional push-up. The position was first described in the 14th century, in the 643-verse Hatha Yoga Pradipika.

In the western world, the exercise gained popularity in the early 20th century, particularly in the military. The Israeli Army's Bar-Or test requires soldiers to do 40 push-ups (with no time limit), while special forces like the American Navy Seals have to do 80 push-ups in two minutes. In the Finnish special force laskuvarjojääkäri it is around 48 in 60 seconds. In some countries, including Switzerland, the military don't do traditional push-ups any more. Instead they do the 'plank', designed to improve core stability.

THE TEST

Men get into the 'military' push-up position: hands and tips of toes on the floor, hands level with the shoulders, fingers pointing forward, arms fully stretched, feet close together, the back straight, elbows as close as possible to the body, butt cheeks clenched. Then bend both arms at the same time and let the upper body sink until it is 15 centimetres above the floor or until the upper arms are parallel to the floor. Women do the same but leave their knees on the floor.

GOOD TO KNOW

1 – Push-ups require 'strength endurance'. This is easier to improve than 'speed strength' (→ Vertical Jump Test, p. 58). With a little training you will soon be able to manage more push-ups. 2 – Fool yourself: only count every second push-up. When you get to 15 you've already done 30. 3 – And how many push-ups can Chuck Norris do? All of them.

Do as many push-ups in a row as you can.

♂ aged	20–29	30–39	40–49	50–59	Over 60
Very good	> 55	> 45	> 40	> 35	> 30
Good	45–55	35–45	30–40	25–35	20–30
Not bad	32–44	22–34	19–29	13–24	10–19
Not great	20–31	15–21	14–18	9–12	7–9
Bad	0–19	0–14	0–13	0–8	0–6

♀ aged	20–29	30–39	40–49	50–59	Over 60
Very good	> 50	> 40	> 35	> 30	> 20
Good	35–50	25–40	20–35	15–30	6–20
Not bad	16–34	13–24	10–19	7–14	4–5
Not great	8–15	6–12	5–9	4–6	2–3
Bad	0–7	0–5	0–4	0–3	0–1

The indications serve only as guidelines. In the Sources you can find links to standardised values.

58

How high can I jump?

WHAT IT'S ABOUT
Playing basketball, at a concert, escaping over a garden fence: there are many occasions when you need to leap in the air. But how can you measure a jump?

THE TEST
The most popular method of measurement is the Vertical Jump Test. Stand side-on to a high wall. With shoulders pulled back, reach up with your dominant arm (→ Handedness Test, p. 72), making sure this arm is closest to the wall. The point at which your fingertips touch the wall is where the measurement starts and is called the standing reach height. A helper can mark the spot with a piece of chalk or tape. Now jump up as high as you can. You are allowed to bend your knees and pick up momentum by swinging your arms. With your fingertips, touch the wall at the highest possible point (you can dust your fingertips with chalk so that they leave a mark on the wall).

HOW IT'S EVALUATED
To get your Vertical Jump result, measure the distance between the bottom and top mark on the wall. Base your result on the best of three jumps. In the 2012 NBA pre-drafts, Harrison Barnes jumped 96.5 centimetres from a standing reach.
☛ Don't be too hopeful that with a bit of intensive training you'll manage a slam dunk. Because bounce is due to elasticity (springiness) it will take a little time to train to achieve your goals.

GOOD TO KNOW

A good justification for those who can't jump that high is the Lewis formula:
Average power (Watts) = $\sqrt{4.9 \times 9.81}$ x weight x $\sqrt{\text{jump-reach score in metres} \times 9.81}$
The heavier a person is, the more body mass he needs to move when jumping.
So at least a heavy person achieves his worse result with more effort.

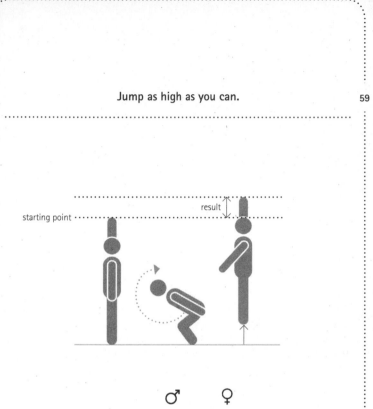

	♂	♀
Excellent	> 50	> 40
Good	35–50	25–40
Not bad	16–34	13–24
Not great	8–15	6–12
Bad	0–7	0–5

60 How much stamina do I have?

WHAT IT'S ABOUT

Our muscles are supplied with energy in two ways: aerobically and anaerobically. Aerobic means 'with oxygen': the more air we breathe in, the more oxygen we consume, the more energy we release. So if you can still speak while running, you are in the aerobic zone, because speaking requires normal breathing, which in turn is a prerequisite for an aerobic supply of energy. The anaerobic energy supply is released under heavy strain – in a sprint, for example. This only works for a short time before you start to gasp for air. Your body forces you to switch back to an aerobic energy supply.

THE TEST

In 1968 the army doctor Kenneth Cooper developed a simple process to test the aerobic fitness level of recruits. He let them run for 12 minutes and saw how far they got. The test and Cooper's book *Aerobics* marked the start of the jogging mania that is still going strong. Before this, jogging was still called running and was exhausting; now suddenly it was healthy. But whether or not the measured value resulting from the Cooper test is a reliable indication of fitness is a moot point, as it does not give any information about the actual physical stress on the muscles.

THE EVALUATION

The average for a 40-year-old male is 2,000 metres, the French Foreign Legion expects new recruits to run 2,800 metres, and the world record is 4,753 metres. For details, see the opposite page.

―――――――――― GOOD TO KNOW ――――――――――

Inexperienced endurance athletes often have problems with the Cooper test. The trick is to run at the anaerobic threshold (AT), the point at which you push your body to the maximum, without overexerting yourself. But a person does not have a sense of his AT. We don't notice when we're at the brink, but only when we're already over it. The AT can be reliably measured with a lactate or exercise test.

**Run for 12 minutes on a 400-metre track and compare your
performance with the table below.**

♂ aged	20–29	30–39	40–49	50 +
Very good	> 2800 m	> 2700 m	> 2500 m	> 2400 m
Good	2401–2800 m	2301–2700 m	2101–2500 m	2001–2400 m
Not bad	2201–2400 m	1901–2300 m	1701–2100 m	1601–2000 m
Not great	1600–2200 m	1500–1900 m	1400–1700 m	1300–1600 m
Bad	< 1600 m	< 1500 m	< 1400 m	< 1300 m

♀ aged	20–29	30–39	40–49	50 +
Very good	> 2700 m	> 2500 m	> 2300 m	> 2200 m
Good	2201–2700 m	2001–2500 m	1901–2300 m	1701–2200 m
Not bad	1801–2200 m	1701–2000 m	1501–1900 m	1401–1700 m
Not great	1500–1800 m	1400–1700 m	1200–1500 m	1100–1400 m
Bad	< 1500 m	< 1400 m	< 1200 m	< 1100 m

62

How good is my balance?

THE SUBJECT

The Swiss sport scientist Dr Thomas Wyss carried out a study in which he proved that there is a connection between our coordination skills and our risk of injury. In other words, somebody who does not train his ability to balance is twice as likely to suffer an injury.

THE TEST

The stork test (balancing on one leg) measures the amount of time you are able to stay balanced on one leg. Sounds easy? Try it out.

Take off your shoes and socks. Stand on a flat surface, with your hands on your hips. Place your right leg at an angle, and then rest your foot against your left knee (see diagram on the opposite page). Now stand on the balls of your left foot, i.e. on tiptoe. As soon as you are in this position you can start timing. How long can you hold this position? As soon as you have to take your hands from your hips,

start hopping on your toes, or feel your right foot slipping away from the left knee, time's up. Repeat, balancing on your right leg. Add up the two times.

HOW IT'S EVALUATED

Compare your time with those in the table. The same applies to this exercise as to most others – the more you practise, the better you get. If you're already an expert balancer you can take it to the next level: close your eyes while standing on one leg and slowly tip your head backwards.

GOOD TO KNOW

When balancing on one leg, focus on a point about two metres in front of you on the floor.

	♂	♀
Very good	> 50 sec.	> 30 sec.
Good	41–50 sec.	26–30 sec.
Not bad	31–40 sec.	16–25 sec.
Not great	20–30 sec.	10–15 sec.
Bad	< 20 sec.	< 10 sec.

The indications are guidelines only. In the Sources you can find links to standardised values.

64

How fast can I react?

THE SUBJECT

A reaction time is the amount of time between something happening and our reaction to it. Let's take a well-known example: You are sitting in a car. You can see that the person in the car in front is braking, so you also apply the brake. The period of time between seeing and braking is the reaction time. In a car, a reaction time of 0.2 to 0.3 seconds is considered fast, but it slows down under the influence of drugs or alcohol and also with tiredness, agitation and stress.

THE TEST

Sit on a chair and place your lower arm on the edge of a table in such a way that your hand reaches over the table edge. Another person holds a 30-cm-long ruler between your thumb and index finger (the zero centimetre line of the ruler should be level with the top of your thumb, your other fingers shouldn't touch the ruler). Without any warning, the tester lets go of the ruler. Catch it as quickly as you can between index finger and thumb. Record the distance between the zero-centimetre line of the ruler and the top of the thumb where the ruler has been caught. Repeat the test five times and then work out the average distance. The test measures how quickly you can transmit an impulse from the eye to the brain.

HOW IT'S EVALUATED

Compare your result with the values in the table opposite. A reaction time of under 0.1 seconds (= 5 cm) is taken as 'anticipation' (you reacted before the tester even dropped the ruler) and is deemed a false start.

--- GOOD TO KNOW ---

In his 100-metre world record, Usain Bolt had a reaction time of 0.146 seconds. In a ruler test this would be 10.5 cm. You can test your finger click reaction time online: www.humanbenchmark.com

Very fast	5–8 cm
Fast	9–15 cm
Not bad	16–21 cm
Not great	22–28 cm
Slow	> 28 cm

The values in the table are guidelines only and are not standardised.

66

How flexible am I?

WHAT IT'S ABOUT
Along with endurance, strength, speed and coordination, the fifth category for measuring athleticism is agility. When you get to the stage of having to put your feet on a chair to tie your laces, you'll know why.

THE TEST
The Sit-and-Reach test measures the flexibility of the muscles at the back of your thighs and your lower back muscles. The flexibility of these two muscle groups gives an indication of whether you are at risk of suffering increasingly from back pain.

This is how it works: Do a warm-up. Take your shoes off. Sit on the floor close to a wall. Stretch your legs so that the soles of your feet are flat against the wall. Now try and touch the wall with your hands, keeping your legs stretched. Reach your arms forward as far as you can, hold this position for two seconds.

Repeat the exercise three times and check your performance in the table (→ right page).

ANOTHER TEST
For the Backscratch test you first have to warm up your shoulders and neck area. Then place your right arm behind your head and with the palm of your hand, reach between your shoulder blades and as far as you can down your back. Place your left hand behind your back, palm facing outwards, and reach up as far as possible, attempting to touch the fingertips of both hands. If you can't make them touch, ask somebody to measure the distance between the fingertips. Count the best of two attempts and repeat the procedure with the other shoulder. Check your performance opposite.

--- GOOD TO KNOW ---

In the Sit-and-Reach test, don't try to stretch your arms forward. Try to raise your lower back and then tip forwards. Think 'high' and not 'far'.

Sit-and-Reach Test

Reach	Flexibility
Very good	You can place the whole palm of your hand on the wall.
Good	You can touch the wall with your knuckles.
Not bad	You can touch the walls with your fingertips.
Not great	You can't quite reach the wall.
Bad	You can only reach to your shins.

Backscratch Test

Reach	Flexibility
Very good	You can interlink your fingers.
Good	Your fingertips touch.
Not bad	Your fingertips are less than 5 cm apart.
Not great	Your fingertips are 5 to 15 cm apart.
Bad	Your fingertips are more than 15 cm apart.

The values in the table are guidelines only. You can find links to standardised values in the Sources.

⁶⁸ How sensitive to pain am I?

WHAT IT'S ABOUT

Historically, there are three interpretations of pain:

1 – Pain as a punishment from the gods. In early civilizations, pain was usually thought to be the work of demons. Up to the 17th century, people believed that pain was a consequence of original sin, and a way of sharing Christ's suffering on the cross.

2 – Pain as an expression of weakness. If you can't take pain, then you don't belong. This interpretation of pain is known from initiation rituals of indigenous people. For example, the young men of the Brazilian Sateré-Mawé tribe have to keep their hand in a glove made from leaves filled with highly venomous giant ants for several minutes without screaming.

3 – Pain as a warning signal from the body. We now know that pain can be understood positively. Even though it is disruptive, it is the body's way of telling us that something is wrong.

THE TEST

To this day, pain cannot be measured, and doctors have to rely on patients' descriptions. However, it is possible to measure our pain threshold and our tolerance to pain. A famous method is the ice-water test, which involves holding your hand in icy water and measuring two intervals: the time between plunging your hand into the water to the moment when you start to feel pain measures your pain threshold, and the time from that point to the moment when you can't bear it any more and pull your hand out measures your pain tolerance.

--- GOOD TO KNOW ---

Pain tolerance can be manipulated. If the ice-water experiment is carried out by an attractive person, we are able to keep our hand in the water considerably longer. Loud swearing, roaring with laughter and regular practice also increase tolerance.

How long can you bear it?

Fill a container with ice-cubes and add cold water. Wait for five minutes, then plunge your hand into the water.

⚠ Do not leave your hand in the ice water for longer than two minutes!

< 40 seconds = very sensitive
40–60 seconds = average
> 60 seconds = not at all sensitive

70

Do I need (new) glasses?

WHAT IT'S ABOUT

The ancient Egyptians had magnifying glasses (or 'meniscal lenses'), while the first spectacles were developed in Venice at the end of the 13th century. But it was only in 1862 that an assistant doctor at the eye hospital in Utrecht answered the rather obvious question: From what point on do we need glasses?

THE TEST

Hermann Snellen developed a method for measuring a person's eyesight by getting the test person to recognise letters. Your eyesight is bad from the moment that you can no longer tell an O from a C, or when an E looks no different from an F. To define this exact moment, he asked test persons to read out differently sized letters from a specific distance. He did not use a standard font for the letters, but developed his own – the optotype.

HOW IT'S EVALUATED

Those who could easily read the 8.7-millimetre-high letters from a distance of 6 metres (20 feet) had normal vision. This 20/20 rule is still the norm for good eyesight today.

Snellen's eye chart, often called the Snellen Chart, became the standard means for measuring visual acuity. In 1868 he developed the 'tumbling E' chart, in which the test person had to indicate which way the letter E was facing. It is based on the same principle as the normal chart but is used for children and illiterate adults.

To this day, the Snellen Chart is the bestselling poster in the USA.

GOOD TO KNOW

What do these four statements have in common?
1. Sitting too close to the TV is bad for your eyes. 2. Reading under the covers with a torch is bad for your eyes. 3. Eating carrots helps you see in the dark. 4. People who wear glasses can't become pilots. Answer: They are all wrong.

Place this book on a table so that you can see the chart in good light. Sit on a chair exactly 1.5 metres away (from the book to your eyes). Cover one eye: Which line can't you read completely? Repeat with the other eye.

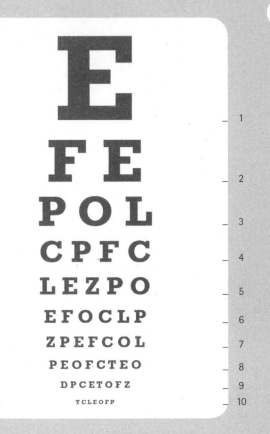

If you can read all eight lines, then you have perfect eyesight (Visual acuity = 1.0). If you made mistakes, a visit to the optician is advisable.

These results are suggestions. This test is not a substitute for a standardised, professional diagnosis.

72

Am I left-handed?

WHAT IT'S ABOUT

There are more myths about left-handed people than there are about 9/11. A quick clarification:

1 – **Left-handed people are cleverer than right-handed people.** Wrong. Well, almost. The average IQ (→ IQ Test, p. 120) is the same for both, but differently distributed. There are more left-handed people with learning difficulties, but also more who are highly intelligent.

2 – **Left-handed people are more creative than right-handed people.** True. Left-handed people are more likely to have a creative job. And they tend to suffer more from respiratory problems, stutter more, are more often homosexual, are more often top-class athletes, and earn more after graduating.

3 – **We don't know why people are either left-handed or right-handed.** True. It is assumed that handedness is genetic, but the gene has not yet been found. (→ Gene Test, p. 82)

4 – **One in ten people are left-handed.** False. In surveys, 10 to 15 per cent claimed to be left-handed, but targeted tests show that a bigger group is ambidextrous. Many of these have a 'preference' but no 'pure' handedness.

THE TEST

There are countless methods for determining handedness. In Asia, it is established with a simple question: in which hand do you hold your chopsticks? When buying this book, with which hand did you take it off the shelf?

Interestingly, it is not only our hands that have a left/right preference. To determine the dominant eye, a test person is made to look through a keyhole; while the dominant ear is determined with a telephone test, i.e. to which ear does the person hold the phone.

GOOD TO KNOW

Surfers and skaters know the Goofy Test for finding out your natural stance: Ask a friend to give you a light shove from behind. The leg on which you lunge forward is the leg that you should have at the front of the board. Left = regular, right = goofy

Mark with a cross the answer that applies to you.

	always with my left hand	usually with my left hand	sometimes left hand, sometimes right	usually with my right hand	always with my right hand
I write ...	☐	☐	☐	☐	☐
I hold a knife (without fork) ...	☐	☐	☐	☐	☐
I brush my teeth ...	☐	☐	☐	☐	☐
I hold a spoon ...	☐	☐	☐	☐	☐
I light a match ...	☐	☐	☐	☐	☐
I steer a computer mouse ...	☐	☐	☐	☐	☐
	x (-50)	x (-25)	x 0	x 25	x 50
Total per column	☐	☐	☐	☐	☐

Add up the number of crosses per column. Multiply this number by the factor at the bottom of the column (e.g. 3 crosses in the column 'always with my left hand' multiplied by -50 = -150 points). Then add up the scores from each column and divide the total by three. You will get a lateral quotient of between -100 and +100.

-100	-50	0	+50	+100
totally left-handed	primarily left-handed	totally ambidextrous	primarily right-handed	totally right-handed

Based on the Edinburgh Handedness Inventory (revised), not standardised.

74

Which side of my brain do I think with?

WHAT IT'S ABOUT

Our brain is made up of two halves (hemispheres) that each control the opposite side of the body. The division of labour between the two halves of the brain is called lateralisation. There are a number of reliable indications that the two sides fulfil different tasks. But it is not the case that our brain consists of an 'analytical' left side and a 'creative' right, of 'theory and practice', 'man and woman', 'yin and yang'. It is more complicated than that.

THE TEST

Contrary to what you might read on the Internet, there is no *one* test that can determine whether the left or the right side of the brain is dominant. There are only many different tests that can determine which brain functions are dominated by the left or the right side of the brain. Some of these tests are listed opposite.

HOW IT'S EVALUATED

The right hemisphere is responsible for the big picture: it puts things in context, reads between the lines, recognises body language and individuals, not just categories. The left side is more focused on detail, provides clarity, and mechanically uses tools and words that we already know. According to the psychiatrist and brain expert Iain McGilchrist, we have created a world that is aligned more with the left side of the brain: it is technical, bureaucratic, virtual, controlled, and logical. However, this left–right division is not as clear as we might like to believe, there is in fact a lot of overlap between the two. The two halves of the brain give us two different pictures of the world that we combine into one.

GOOD TO KNOW

'Besides, I think with my knee.' *Joseph Beuys*

Answer the following questions.

1. Fold your hands. Which thumb is on top?

   A ☐ Right thumb
   B ☐ Left thumb

2. Draw a straight line on the ground and walk along it with your eyes closed. Open your eyes. In which direction have you diverted from the line?

   A ☐ To the right
   B ☐ To the left

3. Look at your computer desktop. What state is it in?

   A ☐ Tidy and organised
   B ☐ Chaotic

4. Draw a Q on your forehead with your finger. How did you draw it?

   A ☐ So that the viewer can read it on your forehead
   B ☐ So that you can read it

5. Look at an object in front of you. Now close one eye. Which one did you close?

   A ☐ Left eye
   B ☐ Right eye

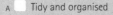

Count up your As and Bs.

More As indicates a left dominance, more Bs a right dominance.

76

What is my dosha?

WHAT IT'S ABOUT

The Vedas, one of the oldest bodies of texts in the world, contained the secrets of the Brahmins, members of the highest priestly caste of Hinduism, including the knowledge of how to live a long life: Ayurveda. These 5,000-year-old medical teachings cover the physical, mental, social and spiritual aspects of life, based around three main constitutions: Vata, Pitta and Kapha, known as the three doshas. Establishing a patient's constitution is the starting point of an Ayurvedic anamnesis before beginning a treatment.

THE TEST

Ascertaining Vata, Pitta and Kapha by means of a mundane questionnaire (→ right page) corresponds more to a Western approach. The traditional Indian anamnesis is based on a complicated pulse diagnosis. For men, the pulse is measured on the right wrist, for women on the left. **Vata**: pulse like a snake (fast), **Pitta**: pulse like a frog or a crow (medium speed), **Kapha**: pulse like a swan (slow).

HOW IT'S EVALUATED

Few people are 'pure' types. Usually two aspects are present in roughly equal measure.

A – Vata: You are lively, smart, cheerful and popular, but also nervous, volatile and easily bored. You sleep badly, and are prone to respiratory and joint problems. You have a slim, light build.

B – Pitta: You have a large appetite and a sharp intellect with a slight tendency to being over-critical. You are enthusiastic and passionate. You are prone to nervous stomach problems.

C – Kapha: You are balanced and relaxed. Your slow powers of comprehension are countered by a good long-term memory. You have a powerful build and thick hair. You are a good sleeper. You are prone to weight problems.

——————— GOOD TO KNOW ———————

You cannot change your basic constitution. The goal is to balance out your doshas through diet, meditation and the right lifestyle.

Mark with a cross the descriptions that apply to you.

....

Build

A   Light, diminutive, lose weight when stressed
B   Medium weight, muscular
C   Strongly built, prone to being overweight

Appetite

A   Changeable, forget to eat, picky
B   Can eat anything, all the time
C   Balanced, can easily skip a meal or fast

Sweat

A   Don't sweat much, little odour
B   Sweat a lot, sweat sometimes has a strong odour
C   Medium, sweat has a cooling effect, sweat sometimes smells sweet (but pleasant)

Sexuality

A   Inconsistent, strong desire but little sexual energy, playful
B   Moderate sexual desire, passionate, tend towards dominance
C   Low but constant sexual desire, adapt to my partner's sexuality

Beliefs/Convictions

A   Volatile, changeable, spontaneous
B   Constant, committed, can become fanatical
C   Steady, gentle, maintain basic values, trust in the flow of life

Spirit

A   Active, curious, clear, fast, adaptable, indecisive
B   Intelligent, critical, analytical, decisive, proactive
C   Calm, deliberate, slow to make decisions but stick to them

Sleep

A   Light, refreshing, can get up early, prone to insomnia
B   Medium, deep, quick to fall back to sleep if woken in the night
C   Deep, like to sleep a long time, not a morning person

....

Count up your points. Which type dominates?

A = Vata   B = Pitta   C = Kapha

Am I a human?

WHAT IT'S ABOUT
What distinguishes me from an animal? This is a good conversation starter if you find yourself sitting next to a theologian, biologist or philosopher at a dinner party.

THE TEST
One of the best methods for distinguishing between lower and higher forms of life is the mirror test. Being able to recognise your reflection is a sign of cognitive superiority. This thesis dates back to the 1970s, when psychologists developed the 'rouge test', which involves marking the forehead of a child or the fur of an animal with red ink. Only animals that recognise their own reflection remove the smudge. Cats and dogs don't pass the test. Chimpanzees, elephants and dolphins do. The only non-mammals to recognise themselves are crows and magpies.

HOW IT'S EVALUATED
6–12 months: Curiosity. Babies crawl towards the mirror to try and make contact with the 'other baby'.
13–24 months: Aversion. Babies of this age react more cautiously, smile shyly at most, or look behind the mirror for the 'other baby'. Some psychologists see this as a first sign of self-awareness, as the baby defines itself in relation to another.
From 20 to 24 months: Me! By the age of two, all humans pass this test and recognise themselves in the mirror.

———————————— GOOD TO KNOW ————————————

For all concerned parents: The age at which a child first masters the mirror test has nothing to do with the baby's intelligence. The French psychoanalyst Jacques Lacan describes the 'mirror stage' as a dialectical process, in which the child learns to differentiate between the inner and the outer world, and also as the beginning of narcissism: the child learns that 'I is another' – the first of many narcissistic self-delusions (→ Narcissism Test, p. 26).

80

Do my parents have dementia?

THE SUBJECT

Some things get better with age. Our vocabulary increases, we become more compassionate ('softening with age'), we are happier with our sexuality, and we're not as stressed. Other things, including our brainpower, get worse. It already begins in our late twenties, when our prefrontal cortex – in other words, our brain – begins to shrink. Humans are the only beings to whom this happens, and they are the only ones to suffer from Alzheimer's, a form of dementia. A 2011 study found out that fear of losing our minds is greater than our fear of death. There is no medication that can cure Alzheimer's, although there are treatments that can slow it down, which is why an early diagnosis is important.

THE TEST

The clock test is a simple and quick method to check if somebody is showing the first signs of dementia. The method is even used by doctors to record the progress of Alzheimer's, and tests two abilities: problem-solving and visuoconstruction – the ability to recognise and reconstruct abstract signs. The clock test is often combined with other screenings in order to assess if there are any early signs of the onset of dementia. The 'Mini Mental State Examination', for example, consists of a series of questions: On what floor of the building are we on? What day of the week is it? Repeat the following three words after me: pen, apple, door. What is 100 minus 7, minus 7 … Which three words did you just repeat after me?

GOOD TO KNOW

What are the three advantages of Alzheimer's?
You can hide your own Easter eggs. You get to know new people every day. You can hide your own Easter eggs.

Draw a big circle on a piece of paper and place it in front of the subject.
Then ask:

**'Draw a clock with all the numbers in the circle
and then mark in the time ten past eleven.'**

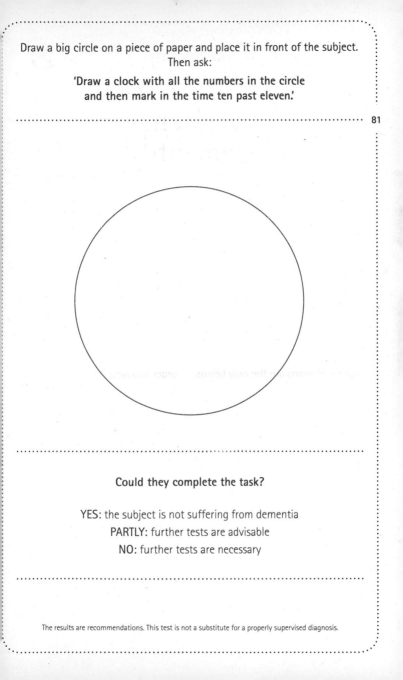

Could they complete the task?

YES: the subject is not suffering from dementia
PARTLY: further tests are advisable
NO: further tests are necessary

82

What does my DNA reveal about me?

WHAT IT'S ABOUT

In principle, our entire genome is decodable and readable. Base pair for base pair, gene for gene, chromosome for chromosome. But readable does not always mean comprehensible, and comprehensible does not always mean useful.

THE TEST

The data required for the test is almost always the same: a saliva sample or a hair, with which the genetic substance of the person being tested can be established unequivocally. In the lab, the sample is processed and the person's DNA is isolated from the cells. Of particular interest are the single-nucleotide polymorphisms (SNPs), i.e. the parts of the DNA that are different in every individual. While around 99 per cent of all base pairs are the same for all people (they are what make us human), the remaining one per cent has another three million positions that can differ from one another – genetically, they are what make us individuals.

HOW IT'S EVALUATED

An individual can be determined by analysing the most important of these SNPs or 'Snips'. Genetic tests are primarily used for making comparisons, for example to prove if the test person is the father of a child (with whose genetic substance the sample is compared), or the perpetrator of a crime (for which a comparison is made with DNA traces from the scene of the crime). In medicine, genetic tests are used, above all, for prenatal diagnostics (does the embryo have a genetic disease?) and for the diagnosis of monogenetic diseases – diseases caused by a defect in a single SNP. There are more than 2,000 known variations of these diseases, and more than 1,000 of them can be established with a genetic test. None of them can be cured – but in many cases the effects of the genetic defect can be limited through a change of lifestyle. Genetic tests for private purposes are highly controversial, i.e. when an analysis of the individual DNA is used to find out 'who you are'. In the past this was done with a horoscope, nowadays with a genetic test.

The market leader for this kind of test is a US company called '23andMe'. Founded in 2006 by Anne Wojcicki (and financed by Google), the biotech start-up began by specialising in genetic tests for private individuals – originally for 999 dollars per person, but now for only 99 dollars for a considerably more comprehensive test. The sequencing of a person's entire genome cost 100 million dollars at the start of the millennium; by the end of the first decade it had already gone down to 50,000 dollars.

THE CRITICISM

The rapid drop in price is part of the problem, because decoding the genome can have unforeseeable consequences. What if the saliva sample indicates that you have a high chance of getting breast cancer or Alzheimer's? These kinds of results can turn your whole life upside down, without adequate preparation.

A consequence of this is that since the end of 2013, '23andMe' is forbidden from giving prognoses of possible genetic diseases. Now they are only allowed to give information about the past, for example how many genes you have in common with Genghis Khan, from what part of the world your ancestors came, or what per cent of your DNA comes from Africa, the cradle of civilisation. However, clients are still provided with the raw data of their tests, which can be analysed with specialised SNP software such as Promethease.

The possibilities of genetic testing are endless. It is not inconceivable that private health insurers will soon select their customers based on genetic tests, or that before we start a family we will want to first check our partner's genetic material. We are only at the very beginning.

──────── GOOD TO KNOW ────────

Can you roll your tongue?
Then your mother or father must be (or have been) a tongue-roller too.
☞ Wrong! Contrary to popular wisdom, the ability to roll one's tongue is not hereditary. In the 1940s it was proven that this simple paternity test is meaningless: 'non-rollers' can also beget 'rollers'.

Skills
& career

●—●—③—●—●

How do I decide?

WHAT IT'S ABOUT

In the 1990s the Swiss sociologist Peter Gross coined the term *Multioptionsgesellschaft*, or multi-option society. His theory is that we have so many choices that they become a burden to us. But not everybody has this problem. Researchers into this topic distinguish between two types of decision-maker: the 'maximiser' and the 'satisfier'. The maximiser asks himself: Is this the best choice? The satisfier asks: Is this the right choice? The maximiser has very high standards, he is a perfectionist who goes out of his way to make the best decision. But he is plagued by self-doubt. He makes a decision, but continues looking. He falls in love, but doesn't delete his profile on Tinder. The satisfier is less demanding. This doesn't mean that he makes do with a mediocre choice. On the contrary, he too may have high standards. But he does not strive for the optimal result, he strives to fulfil his requirements. As soon as he has made a decision, he no longer questions it.

THE TEST

In 2002, the psychologist Barry Schwartz and his team researched the maximisation phenomenon, which was first observed by Herbert Simon in 1956. Schwartz and his team developed the maximisation scale, which measures the level of optimisation in a decision-making process. They compared the results with the test person's happiness (→ Subjective Happiness Scale, p. 146).

HOW IT'S EVALUATED

Objectively, maximisers are better at making decisions than satisfiers, but are no less satisfied with the result. Picture it like this: the more effort you make to reach the right decision, the higher your expectations become. And the higher your expectations, the harder they are to fulfil. Your dissatisfaction increases.

--- GOOD TO KNOW ---

At a restaurant, as soon as you find a dish that appeals to you on the menu, order it. Don't read on – you'll never know what you missed.

To what extent do the following statements apply to you?

doesn't apply at all   (1) (2) (3) (4) (5) (6) (7)   applies completely

1. Regardless of how happy I am in my job, I always keep my eyes open for a better opportunity.

2. When I listen to the radio in the car, I often change the station. I want to know if something better is playing somewhere else – even if I like what I'm currently listening to.

3. I find it difficult to find gifts for friends.

4. In the video shop (or Netflix etc.) I find it difficult to choose the right film.

5. I am never satisfied with second best.

6. I have very high standards in everything I do.

Add up your points and divide the total by 6.

Your result:

Brief analysis: < 4 = you are a satisfier   ≥ 4 = you are a maximiser

You can find more information on the normal distribution of the 13-question version of the Maximisation Scale in the Sources.

With the kind permission of Barry Schwarz et. al.

How do I learn best?

WHAT IT'S ABOUT

Failures and misadventures at school are a topic that always get the conversation going: 'I was crap at maths', or 'I hated French', or 'My three-year old sister could draw better than me!' Victories are good for the soul, defeats make good stories. Perhaps you really didn't have a talent for a particular subject – or perhaps you were just taught it in the wrong way. We are not talking here about bad teachers, but about different learning types.

THE TEST

In 1987, Neil Fleming developed the pioneering VARK® test to determine personal learning preferences. Although the validity of the test has been frequently challenged, it is still one of the most popular methods for identifying learning types.

HOW IT'S EVALUATED

According to the test, there are four different learning types:

Visual type: You learn through observation. You use diagrams and models to visualise your ideas. You replace key words with symbols. You use coloured marker pens.

Auditory type: You learn through listening. You ask questions. You discuss the topics you have to learn with others, or present your topic in the form of a mini-lecture.

Writing and reading type: You learn through texts. You gain clarity by writing things down. You add your own comments when taking notes and reformulate important bits.

Kinaesthetic type: You learn by trying. You use practical examples to explain your concepts. You try to remember experiences instead of facts.

GOOD TO KNOW

When we lose something we try and remember when we last used it. This context-dependent memory can be used in learning. Research carried out at the University of Iowa shows that students get better grades if they take their exam in the same place where they revised for it.

In each section, choose the answer that best describes your approach.
☞ Choosing more than one answer is allowed

....

1. You are given the menu in a restaurant. How do you decide?

   R ☐ You choose a dish based on the description
   K ☐ You order something you've had here before
   V ☐ You look at what people on neighbouring tables are having
   A ☐ You ask the waiter or the person you are with to help you make a
   decision

2. Do you prefer a teacher or trainer who likes to ...

   R ☐ use hand-outs and/or textbooks?
   V ☐ use flow-charts, pictures and films?
   K ☐ organise field-trips or work-experience placements?
   A ☐ have discussions and invite guest speakers?

3. You buy a new digital camera. What, apart from the price, most
   influences your decision?

   R ☐ The features of the camera, which you have informed yourself about
   in the manual or online
   A ☐ The salesperson who explained the features to you
   V ☐ The design of the camera, which you find appealing
   K ☐ The test that you put the camera through

....

Which letters did you choose?

V = Visual type A = Auditory type R = Reading and writing type
K = Kinaesthetic type

This text is an excerpt. The original questionnaire can be found on:
www.vark-learn.com

....

With the kind permission of Neil D. Fleming.
© Copyright version 7.3 (2001), Neil D. Fleming, Christchurch, New Zealand

90

Do I have good concentration?

WHAT IT'S ABOUT
Concentration is the relationship of speed to precision. It is about being fast without becoming sloppy, doing things thoroughly without getting lost in the details.

THE TEST
There are a variety of standardised methods: FAIR (Frankfurt Attention Inventory), Abel's Test, the Cambridge Brain Sciences test and the classic, the d2. This test is astonishingly reliable despite the apparently trivial task that it sets. Meta-studies show a high correlation between the result and actual concentration outside the test situation. Our example is a short version of the d2. It works like this: On the right, find all d2s, i.e. all letter ds marked with two lines, which could be in any of the following forms:

Distractors make the task more difficult:

d d d d d   p p p p p

Start in the top left-hand corner and search for the d2s, line by line. Cross through each one you find and stop after 60 seconds.

HOW IT'S EVALUATED
1 – Speed: How far did you get? Every line has 32 characters. (The numbers at the end of each line make it easier for you to calculate.)
2 – Precision: Go through each line again slowly and mark any mistakes you made (any d2s that you missed, or mistakenly marked distractors).
3 – Result: Insert your speed and precision values in the matrix to get your result. You would most probably get the same result if you did the real d2 test.

GOOD TO KNOW

'Look three times, act once. Young people don't always get this. Slow and accurate is better than fast and for the last time.' *Sten Nadolny*

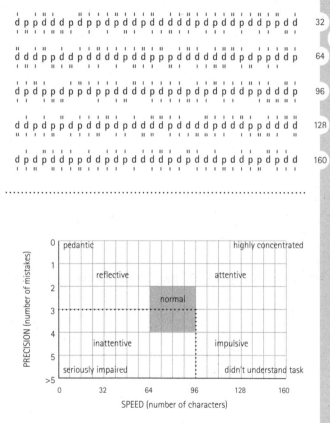

Plotted example: 3 mistakes (precision) and 96 characters (speed).

With the friendly assistance of Hogrefe Verlag GmbH & Co. KG.

How fast can I read?

WHAT IT'S ABOUT

Thesis: we read differently online than offline. Instead of reading everything, we scan the page in an F-pattern. We read the first line, then jump vertically to the next paragraph, read the first line and then jump to the end of the text. The reason: normal reading isn't fast enough for us. The result: We don't take away much from our reading. Perhaps – and this is just a suggestion – we should learn to read faster.

THE TEST

The text on the right-hand page is the test. Before you read it, make sure you have a stopwatch or phone with a timer function to hand. Count down 60 seconds before you start reading. Read as fast as possible, but read thoroughly – you will be asked questions about the text.

Ready, steady, go!

HOW IT'S EVALUATED

First answer these control questions. No cheating please!

1 – What does wpm mean?
2 – How many words does the text have?
3 – What percentage of the population are fast readers?

Using the scale on the right edge of the text, calculate how many words you read (the numbers indicate the number of words up to the end of the respective lines). For each answer that you got wrong, reduce your number of read words by 20 per cent. The adjusted result is your wpm.

50-75 wpm: you read like a third-grader. 75-150 wpm: you read like an eighth-grader. 150-250 wpm: you read like an average adult. 250-300 wpm: You read like a student. >4,700 wpm: you've just broken the world record.

--- GOOD TO KNOW ---

There is of course an app for this. The company Spritz has developed a technology whereby only one word appears on the screen at a time. The speed can be increased to 600 wpm. You could then read *Lord of the Rings* in 13 hours.

The number of words that you read in one minute is your — 12
reading speed. A normal reading speed is around 200 words — 22
per minute (wpm) and depends on reading ability and on the — 33
complexity of the text. This text has around 340 words. So if — 44
you read the whole text in one minute, your reading speed — 55
is above average. But that does not mean much unless you — 66
understand what you read. On average, we understand 60 per — 76
cent of a text. So if you read 200 words in a minute and your — 91
text comprehension is average, then your real reading speed — 100
is 60 per cent of 200, so 120 words per minute. Experienced — 112
speed-readers, which account for only one per cent of the — 123
population, read 1,000 words per minute and have a reading — 133
comprehension of 85 per cent. The real reading speed is then — 144
85 per cent of 1,000 = 850 wpm. But why do some people — 157
read faster than others? The key words here are 'eye move- — 168
ment' and 'subvocalisation'. Most readers 'fixate' a line of text — 178
with five to six eye movements. The trick of speed-readers is — 190
to make fewer fixations and thereby to grasp bigger groups of — 203
words. You intuit the meaning of a sentence even if you don't — 215
read every word. Subvocalisation is what children do when — 224
they learn to read – they read the words under their breath. — 235
With this method, words are not grouped together because — 244
you 'read out' every single word. Critics of speed-reading — 254
argue that subvocalisation is necessary to follow complicated — 262
trains of thought in a text and above all in order to remember — 275
everything. Speed-reading does not have much to do with — 285
reading for pleasure. To skim through a good book at 450 wpm — 297
is about as satisfying as slinging down a three-course meal in a — 310
top restaurant in the space of ten minutes. Speed-readers like — 321
to claim that most of what we read is neither difficult to under- — 334
stand nor done for pleasure. — 339

Can I write well?

WHAT IT'S ABOUT

When it comes down to it, there are two types of people – talkers and writers. The former express themselves better verbally (they think as they talk), the latter need the peace and solitude of a sheet of white paper (they think as they write). But even the talkers would like to be good writers. Love letters, emails, Facebook posts, Tweets – we write all the time.

Here are a few little pearls of wisdom from great writers including Arthur Schopenhauer, George Orwell and journalist Constantin Seibt:

1 – **Short words are better.** Don't write 'discombobulated', write 'confused'. Don't give a 'concrete example', give an 'example'.

2 – **Keep it brief.** Long sentences are easy to write but hard to read. Stick to one thought per sentence.

3 – **Avoid jargon.** Terms like 'shifting paradigms', 'leverage' or 'synergise' will only be understood by insiders.

4 – **Read every text you write out** loud before sending it off. If something sounds awkward, it is also awkward to read.

5 – **Break all of these rules.**

Copywriting is one of the most concise and creative forms of writing. David Ogilvy, often hailed as the father of advertising, claimed that you 'can't bore people into buying your product'. Ideally, advertising messages are polished, entertaining, seductive – and break their own rules. Like the *Economist*'s billboard ad: 'A poster should contain no more than eight words, which is the maximum the average reader can take in at a single glance. This, however, is a poster for Economist readers.'

THE TEST

To become a copywriter you may have to pass a copy test. On the right is an example based on the copy test of the major German advertising agency Springer & Jacoby.

GOOD TO KNOW

If you wouldn't say it, don't write it.

Qualitative evaluation:

Ask somebody whom you consider to be a good copywriter to evaluate what you've written using school grades.

Competition evaluation:

Ask somebody whom you consider to be a good copywriter to write his or her own text for the sign. Compare.

Quantitative evaluation:

Write your sentence on a big piece of cardboard, sit with it for two hours on the high street and see how much money you get.

Am I creative?

WHAT IT'S ABOUT
There is a lot of academic theory surrounding 'creativity', which can be summed up with one question: Is creativity a cat or a dog? Does it keep its distance when you call and only come when it feels like it, or can you train and discipline it? After all, entire industries depend on being able to tap creativity on demand. As yet, researchers into creativity don't have an answer to this question. But they do claim to be able to define what creativity is.

THE TEST
Two well-known methods are the 'Alternative Uses Task' and the 'Tolerance Tests of Creative Thinking'. On the following pages you can see how this technique works, although it should be noted that our versions are not tantamount to a scientific analysis. However, they are tasks that require original solutions and not correct ones. Which, you could say, is a pretty good definition of creativity.

HOW IT'S EVALUATED
1 – Fluency How many different ideas did you have?

2 – Originality How unusual are your suggestions? (word is already out that you can use a paper-clip to remove a SIM card from a smartphone).

3 – Flexibility How many different areas do your ideas cover? (e.g. SIM-card removal and restarting a computer are both mechanical hacks)

4 – Elaboration How precise is your description?

Each response is compared to the total number of responses from all of the people you gave the test to. Higher scores indicate creativity.

GOOD TO KNOW

A trick: quickly down two pints of beer.
In a 2012 study fittingly entitled 'Uncorking the Muse', American researchers found out that our creative facilities are sharper after consuming moderate amounts of alcohol. However, if you want to drink more than two beers, → The Alcoholic Test, p. 50).

Think of some new uses for a paperclip.

🕐 1 min.

☞ On the following page we will test your visual creativity.

98

Title:

....

☞ Evaluate yourself based on the examples and criteria on the right.

Compare the creativity level of your drawing with these examples.

template | obvious | creative

Criteria:
How original is the drawing? How many separate ideas does it contain?
How detailed is it? The title gives an indication of your verbal creativity.

How fast can I type?

WHAT IT'S ABOUT

A brief observation at the start of the 21st century: handwriting is disappearing. Nowadays, most of us only use it for our signature, taking notes and maybe writing lists. We still see it on hand-written menu boards in some restaurants, and occasionally have to decipher it when we get a prescription from the doctor. But even if academics don't tire of proving the link between progress in learning and the use of pen and paper, and even though it is striking how many architects and artists still sketch their ideas on paper, the computer has nonetheless made handwriting almost completely obsolete. Because typewriting is faster, more legible and easier to correct.

THE TEST

Writing speed is measured in wpm (words per minute, just like reading speed, → p. 92).

HOW IT'S EVALUATED

65 wpm is considered good. A trained ten-finger typist can manage 80 wpm or more, while the average speed for two- and three-finger typists is 25 wpm. Handwriting is even slower – it is hard to manage more than 22 wpm. More important than speed, however, is precision. Helena Matouskova from Prague wrote for 30 minutes at a speed of 164 wpm and made just four mistakes – a world record.

GOOD TO KNOW

It's not just about how fast you type, and how many mistakes you make, but also what you write, and when. The 30-second rule works like this: After every meeting, every lecture, every conversation, take 30 seconds to make a note of the most important points. That's it. Sounds easy – even pointless – but it changes everything.

Set a stopwatch on 🕐 60 seconds, or ask somebody to time you.
Open a Word document and copy the following sentence as many
times as you can in one minute.

Hello, I am a little sentence.
Please copy me.

1. Count the words (In Word under *Tools, Word Count*)

2. Now subtract your typos from the result:
    Every mistake counts as one word. Now you have your
    correct wpm.

    Write it down here:

> 35 = below average
35–65 = average
> 65 = above average

Who should I employ?

WHAT IT'S ABOUT

A job interview is a test that we're all familiar with. You have little time and are under a lot of pressure. You want to show yourself in the best light. Essentially, the employer has just two questions: 'Why should we want you?' and 'Why do you want us?' Although often it boils down to your mood and whether you hit it off with the interviewer(s). Those who know how to sell themselves do better in interviews. That's one of the reasons why big companies are increasingly using standardised psychological tests to make an objective evaluation. But some companies are also returning to the old-fashioned interview. Google, for example, uses behavioural interviews.

THE TEST

A behavioural interview is based on two assumptions:

1 – That the past is the best indicator of the future. As an employer you no longer ask 'How would you solve the following situation?' but rather 'Tell me about an instance in which you solved a situation like this one.' The questions are not hypothetical but based on experience. How much professional experience the candidate has is not important; you might also have gained valuable experience in seemingly trivial situations (school, sports club).

2 – Experiences are not right or wrong. You do not ask 'What are your weaknesses?' but instead begin every question with 'Tell me ...' This takes away the pressure of having to give the right answer.

☛ The less people feel the need to perform, the more they reveal about themselves.

GOOD TO KNOW

You can master the behavioural interview with the **S–T–A–R** method: First describe the starting **S**ituation and the **T**ask, then describe what you did (**A**ction) and what this achieved (**R**esult). Important: It is not about telling success stories. It is about showing that you understood the situation and can connect it with one of your own experiences.

Five behavioural questions:

....

1. Have you ever made a mistake? How did you handle it?

   ☞ We all want to learn from our mistakes, but have we ever really done so? When was the last time we actually apologised for something? When did we last repeat a mistake?

2. Tell me about a situation in which you had to solve a very difficult problem.

   ☞ The question provides two kinds of information. First, the candidate describes how he reacted in a real situation and second, you get small but valuable bits of meta-information, e.g. what does the candidate regard as a 'difficult situation'?

3. What people do you find it difficult to work with?

   ☞ Another, somewhat irritating behavioural question that touches on what everyone knows, i.e. that nobody gets on with everybody. The best approach is for the candidate to immediately say which personality types she doesn't get on with, and how she deals with it.

4. When was the last time you did something for the first time?

   ☞ Curiosity is a key ability in order to learn. Everyone thinks that they are curious, but when did the candidate last demonstrate this fact?

5. On a scale of 1 to 10, how would you judge me as an interviewer?

   ☞ Firstly, feedback is interesting for an interviewer; and secondly, you can test how the candidate deals with authority figures. How honest does she dare to be?

104

Am I getting ahead in my career?

WHAT IT'S ABOUT

If it's true that the world is run not by heads of government but by business bosses, it is surely important to ask what criteria are used to select them. Or, in the context of this book, what tests would they have to pass?

For future managers, the MBA (Master of Business Administration) is considered the most important qualification for climbing the corporate ladder – a kind of quick-cycle business studies degree with a focus on key managerial and social leadership skills. But more important than having an MBA is where you did it. With an MBA from a renowned university, even the most obscure CV will make it to the shortlist for top positions in blue-chip companies. An MBA also opens doors into an elite circle of like-minded people who help each other find jobs and gain board positions. It is no coincidence that the Harvard Business School advertises its MBA programme with 'lifelong networking' and not with 'lifelong learning'.

THE TEST

The prerequisite for doing an MBA is the GMAT, the Graduate Management Admission Test. The GMAT is a million-dollar business. One test costs 250 dollars and around 250,000 tests are done each year.

The GMAT takes about three-and-a-half hours and consists of four parts:

1 – **Essay writing** (Analytical Writing Assessment, AWA): The candidate has to argue a point, for example 'Private companies are more successful than public-sector companies.' The essay does not contribute to the final score but is still a requirement. MBA manuals advise 'not to waste any brain cells on the AWA'. (30 minutes)

2 – **Interpreting data sets** (Integrated Reasoning): Here the candidate is tested on her ability to read tables and diagrams. This part of the test was only added in 2012, because in management consultant companies (where most MBA

graduates want to end up), being able to read charts and diagrams is more important than understanding text. This part of the test also does not contribute to the final score – so no stress. (12 questions, 30 minutes)

3 – **Multiple choice** (quantitative): A maths and logic test with questions like this: 16 is what percentage of 128? A: 0.125%, B: 8%, C: 12.5%. D: 12.8%. E: 128%. (37 questions, 75 minutes)

4 – **Multiple choice** (verbal): This tests the candidate's reading comprehension and critical reasoning. In contrast to the IQ test, the questions in the GMAT get more difficult with every correct answer that is given. This decides who will make it to Harvard and who to Hull.

HOW IT'S EVALUATED

The 'Total Scaled Score' lies between 200 and 800, the average is 545. To get a place on one of the most renowned programmes – e.g. Stanford, INSEAD (Paris), Wharton – ideally with a scholarship, you need a score of over 700. Candidates who get over 760, however, are suspected of being social misfits and therefore unsuitable for top positions in the business world.

What does the test prove? Not much. There is no correlation between a person's GMAT score and their success in later life – and also none between a person's GMAT score and their starting salary following their MBA. In fact, GMAT scores have an average correlation factor of 0.48 with first-year MBA grades (where 1.0 indicates a perfect correlation, and 0.0 that there is no relation between the two). So, all in all, the GMAT's prediction ability is middle of the road.

GMAT scoreboard 2013

1.	New Zealand	608	9.	China	582
2.	Singapore	605	10.	South Korea	581
3.	Argentina	591	11.	Switzerland	580
3.	Austria	591	20.	Germany	570
3.	Belgium	591	29.	France	559
6.	Australia	590	38.	Russia	553
6.	England	590	51.	Netherlands	532
8.	Uruguay	587	51.	USA	532

——————————— GOOD TO KNOW ———————————

'In applications I only look at one test result, which correlates most strongly with the applicant's future performance in the job: his A-level (or equivalent) maths grade at secondary school.' *Head of Personnel at a big management consultancy*

What kind of leader am I?

WHAT IT'S ABOUT

Close your eyes for a moment and think of the bosses you have worked for. Who do you remember? Which situations come to mind in which your boss showed leadership qualities?

What 'leadership qualities' are precisely is a matter of dispute. There is only one point that research seems to agree on: the capacity to make courageous decisions in ambiguous situations is one characteristic. But those leaders incapable of persuading participants, their team or other people are ineffective. That's why in most leadership theories, the ability to make decisions is always weighed against the 'people factor'. This incorrectly labelled 'soft skill' does not describe what you achieve but how you achieve it. Or, as the economist Hans Hinterhuber put it in an interview with the German business magazine *brand eins*: 'The fundamental task of leadership is to be interested in people, to help them develop and motivate them to aim higher than they might believe is possible'. This, according to Hinterhuber, should not be confused with management, which is nothing more than 'the optimisation of something that already exists. Leadership is quite different: it creates and shapes the system'.

THE TEST

The Leadership Judgement Indicator (LJI), developed by Michael Lock and Robert Wheeler, investigates firstly whether you have the knack for choosing the appropriate leadership style for a given situation. Then it identifies your personal preferences in all four classic decision-making and leadership styles. The premise that each situation requires a certain leadership style is the core thesis of 'situational leadership'. On the following pages, you will find a short test based on the LJI.

GOOD TO KNOW

'The best leader is the one who is barely noticed by his or her subordinates. When the goals have been reached, people will say, 'We did it ourselves'. *Lao Tzu*

Read the text below and evaluate the alternative courses of action.

You are the sales manager of an Apple Store. Business is booming, the critical Christmas sales season is about to start and you have just taken on four new sales assistants. Across the street, your competitor has just opened a flagship store. Your new employees have less experience than you. And you haven't yet had the chance to make a comprehensive assessment of their strengths and weaknesses. You are currently training them up and they seem to appreciate your experience. But all of a sudden, your CEO wants you to come up with a strategy to react to the competition. How do you proceed? ☛ Evaluate the alternatives.

ALTERNATIVE 1: You create a concept on your own, taking into account all the preconditions.

① — ② — ③ — ④ — ⑤

ALTERNATIVE 2: You inform all the new employees about the preconditions and invite them to create a new concept.

① — ② — ③ — ④ — ⑤

ALTERNATIVE 3: In a meeting, you discuss your concept with the four new employees. You want to find a unanimous solution.

① — ② — ③ — ④ — ⑤

ALTERNATIVE 4: In a meeting, you ask the four new employees for their opinions. You follow up by creating the concept.

① — ② — ③ — ④ — ⑤

ALTERNATIVE 1: directive leadership style   ALTERNATIVE 3: consensual leadership style
ALTERNATIVE 2: delegative leadership style   ALTERNATIVE 4: consultative leadership style

☛ Turn the page to find out which style is the most appropriate.

Which is the right leadership style?

In this invented example, the most appropriate choice would be ALTERNATIVE 1: (directive): the decision has to be made quickly, it is important and, as the boss, all the relevant information is in your hands. The employees appreciate your experience and are likely to accept your decision. ALTERNATIVE 3: (consensual) is the least appropriate leadership style for this scenario. The participants have no experience of these types of situations, time pressure is too great and there's a risk that your leadership skills will not be taken seriously.

Did you judge ALTERNATIVE 1: as appropriate or highly appropriate? ALTERNATIVE 3: as (highly) inappropriate? Then you seem to recognise the right leadership style for the situation – at least in this scenario. But what is the assessment based on? According to the writers of the LJI, the following ten factors play a role in leadership decisions:

Importance	Is this an important decision?
Urgency	Does the decision have to be made quickly?
Level of information	Does the manager have sufficient information to make the decision single-handedly?
Experience	Has the manager already successfully managed similar decision-making situations?
Employee participation	Does the decision-making situation provide good opportunities to develop the participants' skills?
Commitment	Will the participants follow the manager's decision?
Independence	Can the participants solve the problem independently?
Trust	Can the manager trust the participants to resolve the situation in the best possible way?
Potential for conflict	Are major conflicts likely to occur during the process of planning the strategy?

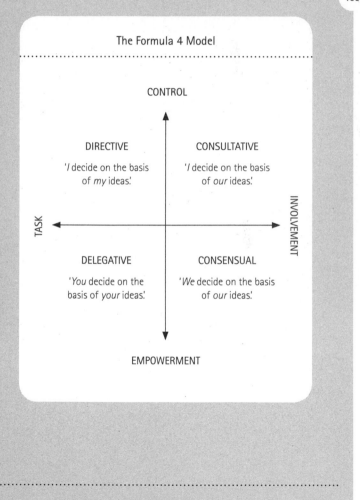

The Formula 4 Model

CONTROL

DIRECTIVE

'*I* decide on the basis of *my* ideas.'

CONSULTATIVE

'*I* decide on the basis of *our* ideas.'

TASK

INVOLVEMENT

DELEGATIVE

'*You* decide on the basis of *your* ideas.'

CONSENSUAL

'*We* decide on the basis of *our* ideas.'

EMPOWERMENT

With the kind permission of the Hofgrefe AG, Verlag Hans Huber

110

Can I motivate myself?

WHAT IT'S ABOUT

On the previous pages, we evaluated your leadership qualities. But one question remains unanswered: Who leads the leader? The answer is: the leader leads him- or herself. Research makes a distinction between three different self-leadership strategies:

1. Behaviour. This refers to the capacity to change one's own behaviour. That doesn't sound like much but it is the core of self-leadership. Let's look at an example: Say that you find it hard to meet deadlines. How do you deal with this? Do you avoid deadlines? Or do you simply accept the fact that you finish projects at the last minute – and suffer each time? Or do you try and change your habits?

2. Rewarding yourself. This refers to the capacity to create situations in which you are motivated. When we enjoy what we do, we feel more competent, more in control, and work feels more meaningful in general. But not all tasks are enjoyable. Therefore, are you in the position to enhance a task, or to block out its negative aspects?

3. Thinking patterns. This refers to the capacity to reshape your own thinking patterns to make them more positive. A good example of this is 'self-talk'. We all imagine important situations that might go wrong. In our heads, we seem to be pessimists. Good self-leadership means: Are you capable of turning destructive, discouraging internal dialogues into positive ones?

THE TEST

Here is a questionnaire written by US researcher Jeff Houghton – the Abbreviated Self-Leadership Questionnaire (ASLQ). It is the short version of the well-known RSLQ, the standard test for examining self-leadership qualities.

GOOD TO KNOW

Here is the short form of the short form: How do you normally reward yourself when you have finished something? And how do you punish yourself if you fail?

How strongly do you agree with these statements?

strongly disagree (1) — (2) — (3) — (4) — (5) strongly agree

1. I work towards specific goals I have set for myself.
2. I establish specific goals for myself and my own performance.
3. I usually keep track of whether I'm doing good work.
4. In difficult situations, I question my views.
5. I visualise myself successfully performing a task before I do it.
6. Sometimes I talk to myself (out loud or in my head) to work through difficult situations.
7. Sometimes I imagine carrying out a task successfully before I actually do it.
8. When I come up against a problem, I question whether my convictions are the right ones.
9. When I have successfully completed a task, I reward myself with something I like.

Add up your score:

> 36 = Very strong self-leadership skills. You have the capacity to influence your behaviour and think positively.

19–36 = Average self-leadership skills. Read through the self-leadership strategies again. Ask yourself: How can I improve myself in these areas?

< 19 = Room for improvement. In your head, go through situations where you did not achieve your goals. Why was that? What role did lack of self-leadership play?

With the kind permission of Jeffery D. Houghton, West Virginia University

How feng shui is my workplace?

WHAT IT'S ABOUT

According to Confucius in the *Book of Rites*, inner harmony is the key to happiness. And it lies buried in the interaction between ourselves and our environment. At the heart of the matter is the idea that the inside and the outside are connected. Those who are helpless, unsuccessful or unhappy should not brood over things in desperation; they should take a careful look at their environment, as the outside helps us draw conclusions about the inside. This may sound like esoteric mumbo-jumbo, yet each one of us knows that when we're in a good phase, we feel better, work more effectively and communicate more clearly. In negative phases, tensions arise, we are tired and we are drawn magnetically to conflicts. Feng shui, the ancient Chinese teaching of harmony in work and life, says that these are not phases, they are zones – physical fields in which our life energy or *qi* flows, or not. What's more, our environment reveals which areas of our life we direct our attention to. A brief example: everything on the right side of your desk symbolises the future – things that you are looking forward to or that you are afraid of. On the left is the past, accumulated issues that you are having difficulty letting go of or incidents that you like thinking about. Right?

THE TEST

An accurate feng shui analysis is as complex as nuclear physics. But the underlying rule is so obvious that it's surprising we break it so often: there is no blanket solution. Change the things that bother you. If you feel good sitting under a motorway bridge, stay there.

GOOD TO KNOW

Your desk is a reflection of your mind. Tidy up before you make decisions. Repair things that are broken.

Quick check: do you have a harmonious workplace?

....

1.	Is your desk tidy?	yes ☐ (1) no ☐ (0)
2.	Do you sit with your back to a door?	yes ☐ (0) no ☐ (1)
3.	Do you sit with your back to a wall?	yes ☐ (1) no ☐ (0)
4.	Do you sit in such a way that you can let your gaze wander (across the room or through the window)?	yes ☐ (1) no ☐ (0)
5.	Do you sit in a draught between the door and the window?	yes ☐ (0) no ☐ (1)
6.	Is your workplace under a sloping roof?	yes ☐ (0) no ☐ (1)
7.	Do you have plants in your room?	yes ☐ (1) no ☐ (0)
8.	Can you see many cables around you?	yes ☐ (0) no ☐ (1)
9.	Do you have a well-organised computer desktop and email box?	yes ☐ (1) no ☐ (0)
10.	Does the building you work in have a harmonious relationship to the neighbouring building?	yes ☐ (1) no ☐ (0)

....

Add up the points (next to the answers).

> 8 points: Your workplace is harmonious. At least according to feng shui criteria.

4–8 points: There is upwards potential. Ask yourself: What does the disharmony say about this stage in your life?

< 4 points: Your workplace is in a *sha qi* zone. No wonder you feel tired and sad there. The first feng shui measure is to tidy up.

114

Am I in the right job?

WHAT IT'S ABOUT

How much do you know about your friends and acquaintances, even those with whom you are only on nodding terms? Presumably you know what jobs they do. After 'How are you?' the most frequently asked question we ask others is: 'What do you do?' The reason lies in our obsessive relationship to work: we define ourselves by what we do for a living and how successful we are at it. But the biggest question remains: Does our everyday work reflect what we are good at?

THE TEST

The test on the following pages is based on the *Bochumer Inventar zur berufsbezogenen Persönlichkeitsbeschreibungen* or BIP (the Bochum Inventory for Job-Related Personality Description) by Rüdiger Hossiep and Michael Paschen. This method covers 14 personality dimensions via self-assessment: attitude to work (conscientiousness, flexibility, ability to take action); professional orientation (motivation to achieve, motivation to create, motivation to lead); social competence (sensitivity, ability to communicate, team orientation, assertiveness) and psychological constitution (emotional stability, resilience, self-confidence).

HOW IT'S EVALUATED

A special feature of job-related methodology is that not only you but also your job is tested. What's interesting is how they match. Do your job-relevant characteristics fit the qualities required for this specific job?

--------- GOOD TO KNOW ---------

Before doing our brief test, it's worth thinking about what Bronnie Ware, a palliative care nurse found out while doing her job. She asked her dying patients: 'What do you regret?' Two of the most common answers were: 1. I wish I'd had the courage to live my own life. 2. I wish I hadn't worked so much.

Rate yourself from 1 (strongly disagree) to 10 (strongly agree).

To follow up, ask your boss to estimate to what extent your job demands the described requirements.

✏ you ✎ your boss

---

1. PROFESSIONAL ORIENTATION

✏ You are strongly committed to a goal and prepared to improve yourself and your performance continually.

✎ The job requires a high motivation to achieve.

| | ✏ | | ✎ | | difference |

✏ You want to shape processes, products and the company.

✎ The job requires a high motivation to shape things, in other words, high involvement.

| | ✏ | | ✎ | | difference |

✏ You want to lead employees and take on leadership responsibilities.

✎ The job requires high motivation to lead.

| | ✏ | | ✎ | | difference |

---

2. ATTITUDE TO WORK

✏ You tend towards perfectionism and are extremely meticulous.

✎ The job requires a high level of conscientiousness.

| | ✏ | | ✎ | | difference |

✏ You are motivated rather than threatened by unclear preliminary situations.

✎ The job requires high flexibility.

| | ✏ | | ✎ | | difference |

✏ You always put decisions into practice immediately.

✎ The job requires a pronounced ability to take action.

| | ✏ | | ✎ | | difference |

3. SOCIAL COMPETENCE

✏️ You sense others' moods and interpret them accurately.
👉 The job demands a high level of sensitivity.

✏️	👉	difference

✏️ You get on well with and are able to deal with other people, and you have many close and casual contacts.
👉 The job requires well-developed interpersonal skills.

✏️	👉	difference

✏️ You are considerate and like harmony.
👉 The job requires a high level of social competence.

✏️	👉	difference

✏️ You enjoy working in a team and prefer collective decisions.
👉 The job requires well-developed teamworking skills.

✏️	👉	difference

✏️ You stand up for your views forcefully and always keep the upper hand.
👉 The job requires a high level of assertiveness.

✏️	👉	difference

4. PSYCHOLOGICAL CONSTITUTION

✏ You are on a very even keel and are able to take failure in your stride.
👁 The job requires a high level of emotional stability.

	✏		👁		difference

✏ You are resistant to stress.
👁 The job requires a high level of resilience.

	✏		👁		difference

✏ You are not bothered by the impression you make on others, and have confidence in yourself.
👁 The job requires a high level of self-confidence.

	✏		👁		difference

1. **For every question, jot down the difference in points between your self-assessment and the job requirements.**

2. **Add up all the differences and divide your result by 14.**

your result:

0-1   High level of agreement. Ask yourself: Have I done the test correctly?

1.1-2.5   Your job fits the job-related personality description. You're probably happy, and so is your boss.

2.6-4   Your job fits the job-related personality description to a large extent. Were there strong deviations on particular points? Why?

4.1-6   Your qualities do not fit the job-related personality description very well. Ask yourself: Why am I doing this job?

> 6   Change your job.

Is my work-life balance in harmony?

WHAT IT'S ABOUT

Fewer and fewer people in Western Europe work full-time. Work psychologists assume that this is a reaction to greater work-related stress (all the way to burnout), as well as the growing number of single parents, steady emancipation from traditional gender roles, and lack of social systems. Some people no longer want to work full-time; others simply cannot because they have to look after children, the sick or the elderly.

The idea of a work-life balance originated in the mid-19th century when child labour began to be restricted. The term became popular during the women's movement.

THE TEST

There are two relevant questions here: How do you measure stress levels? And how do you measure the interaction between work and private life? The Maslach Burnout Inventory (MBI) has prevailed as a standard measurement for depressive exhaustion. Checking your work-life balance is more difficult, however, because the subject of study keeps changing. Twenty years ago, work-life balance referred to the equilibrium between job and leisure time, tension and relaxation – in other words, the capacity to recharge your batteries for work during your leisure time. Today, work-life balance refers to your orientation in the Bermuda triangle of modern responsibilities: job – household – private life. This means that completely new questions are discussed these days: Am I ruining my career chances? What's my employability? In other words, which companies accept my conditions? What should I say 'no' to? And last but not least: Who does what in the household?

--------- GOOD TO KNOW ---------

Part-time work requires discipline and flexibility – but most of all, mental reorganisation.

Answer these questions concerning the last six months.

1. Do you feel that your private life prevents you from investing time in your job in a way that would be helpful to your career? yes ☐ no ☐

2. If you live with a partner: Do both agree on how the housework is divided between you? yes ☐ no ☐

3. Do you feel so exhausted by your work that you find it difficult to get involved with friends and family? yes ☐ no ☐

4. Do private worries have an impact on your performance? yes ☐ no ☐

5. Do you avoid personal contact with colleagues because the exchange is too exhausting? yes ☐ no ☐

6. Do incoming emails or disturbances easily distract you? And do you find it hard to get back to work afterwards? yes ☐ no ☐

7. Do you wake up exhausted? yes ☐ no ☐

8. Do you have to force yourself to go to work although you function well once you are at the office? yes ☐ no ☐

9. Do you feel as if a day at the office gives you a break from family life? yes ☐ no ☐

10. Do you feel restless at work? Does this feeling let up when you're online? yes ☐ no ☐

If you have answered more than three questions with 'yes', you should consider getting some advice.

120

How intelligent am I?

Ever since the Ancient Greeks, the human body has been tested according to all conceivable criteria. The human mind, on the other hand, could only be described in qualitative terms. This changed radically in 1905 when two Frenchmen, Alfred Binet and Théodore Simon, were the first to develop a viable intelligence test. Nowadays intelligence theories assume that there are different kinds of intelligence (often described as verbal, numerical and figural). There is a difference between crystallized intelligence that can grow (vocabulary, knowledge, numeracy, learning and thinking strategies) and fluid intelligence (fast thinking, learning and understanding) that is mainly hereditary but decreases with age. From around the age of thirty, you think somewhat more slowly but compensate for the loss of speed with experience.

THE TEST
There are many different kinds of intelligence test but no single test covers all the subsections of intelligence. Today when we refer to intelligence quotients (IQ) we mean a 1950s standardised procedure that was developed by the US psychologist David Wechsler. The Wechsler IQ test places everyone on a simple grid: an IQ of 100 is the average, whereby half the population is above this level. Highly intelligent people have an IQ of 130, and another two per cent have an IQ lower than 70 – one of the main criteria for a 'mentally disabled' diagnosis.

HOW IT'S EVALUATED
Are you highly intelligent or mentally disabled? Hypothetically speaking, you could be both! The 'Wechsler IQ' compares your performance with a reference group (also known as the norm). If you were compared with 1,000 Albert Einsteins, your IQ could quickly fall below 70. However, if you were compared to 1,000 ten-year-olds, you would automatically be awarded a place in Mensa, the International High IQ Society. Good intelligence tests have several norm tables. This enables you, depending on the question, to be compared with people of the same age, people with the same level of education, or with a norm representation of the

population. Your IQ makes accurate predictions about school or university success and also about your profession. But motivation, personality and other factors also play a role. As a standalone characteristic though, your IQ predicts professional success more accurately than elaborate assessment-centre tests. Admittedly, the connection between having a high IQ and having great career success does not apply across the entire IQ scale: many of the most highly intelligent people do not fit in to the extent that it hinders their careers.

It's interesting that IQ barely changes over the course of a lifetime. Between the first test at the age of six or seven and those at later stages, there is a fluctuation range of plus or minus ten points, no matter what kind of education or training the respective individual has had. This last point is probably the most surprising: school plays almost no role in IQ. When children start primary school, the course of their intelligence has already been set (by their genes, by the influence of parents and carers in infancy, and by their environment). The education system can develop already existing potential – or not (→ Learning Type Test, p. 88). It is important to understand that you can (and should) practise for the test but this will not make you more intelligent. You won't get any better but your result will be more accurate.

THE FLYNN EFFECT
Standardised IQ tests are always changing but their design and evaluation is adjusted to give an average value of 100. Without this 'post-calibration', the results during the course of the 20th century would have got progressively better: today's teenagers would score an average of 20 points higher on an IQ test compared to fifty years ago. The 'Flynn Effect', which was first described in 1984 by James Flynn, a political scientist from New Zealand, does not necessarily mean that we are more intelligent than our grandparents. Two factors are at play here: first, we are much more accustomed to the format of multiple-choice tests today than in the past and we therefore grasp them more easily. And second, the cognitive skills that are examined in an IQ test are more frequently in demand in today's knowledge-based society than in an industrial society. This makes the test less alien to us.

GOOD TO KNOW

IQ tests do not test 'intelligence': they test what is defined as intelligence within the test. Perhaps Hans Magnus Enzensberger was right when he said: 'We're not intelligent enough to know what intelligence is'.

1. WORD FORMATION

Form a word with these letters.
Example: FATRD = DRAFT

🕐 3 min.

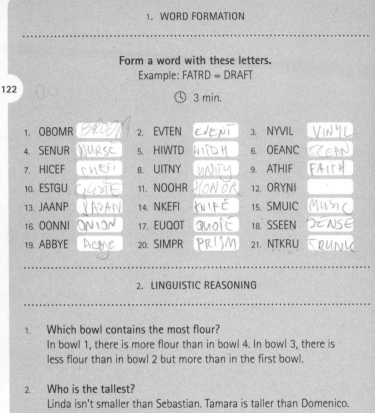

1. OBOMR — *BROOM*
2. EVTEN — *EVENT*
3. NYVIL — *VINYL*
4. SENUR — *NURSE*
5. HIWTD — *WIDTH*
6. OEANC — *OCEAN*
7. HICEF — *CHIEF*
8. UITNY — *UNITY*
9. ATHIF — *FAITH*
10. ESTGU — *GUEST*
11. NOOHR — *HONOR*
12. ORYNI —
13. JAANP — *JAPAN*
14. NKEFI — *KNIFE*
15. SMUIC — *MUSIC*
16. OONNI — *ONION*
17. EUQOT — *QUOTE*
18. SSEEN — *DENSE*
19. ABBYE — *ABBYE*
20. SIMPR — *PRISM*
21. NTKRU — *TRUNK*

2. LINGUISTIC REASONING

1. **Which bowl contains the most flour?**
   In bowl 1, there is more flour than in bowl 4. In bowl 3, there is less flour than in bowl 2 but more than in the first bowl.

2. **Who is the tallest?**
   Linda isn't smaller than Sebastian. Tamara is taller than Domenico. Sabine would be the smallest if it wasn't for Sebastian. Domenico and Linda are the same size.

3. **Who can shout the loudest?**
   Tony shouts more quietly then Heinz. Helmut shouts more loudly than Paul. Paul shouts louder than Heinz. Helmut shouts more loudly than Tony.

3. ANALOGIES

Example: flower : meadow = tree : ?
           forest   wood   nature   root
           (solution: forest)

1. wood : paper = ? : bread
   ☐ cereal   ☐ rye   ☐ corn   ☐ wholewheat

2. word : letter = wall : ?
   ☐ house   ☐ wall   ☐ stone   ☐ fence

3. devil : lived = drawer : ?
   ☐ angel   ☐ reward   ☐ shelf   ☐ died

4. NUMBER SEQUENCES

Which is logically the next figure in this sequence?

Example: 4, 8, 12, 16, 20, ?   Solution: 24 (+4, +4, +4 ...)

A 4, 7, 13, 16, 22, ☐   B 5, 6, 4, 6, 3, 6, ☐   C 20, 15, 45, 41, 123, ☐

Solutions

Word formation: 1. BROOM | 2. EVENT | 3. VINYL | 4. NURSE/RUNES | 5. WIDTH | 6. OCEAN/CANOE | 7. CHIEF | 8. UNITY | 9. FAITH | 10. GUEST | 11. HONOR | 12. IRONY |13. JAPAN | 14. KNIFE | 15. MUSIC | 16. ONION | 17. QUOTE | 18. SENSE | 19. ABBEY | 20. PRISM | 21. TRUNK

Linguistic reasoning: 1. Bowl 2 | 2. Tamara | 3. Helmut |

Analogies: 1. Cereal | 2. Stone | 3. Reward |

Number sequences: Solution A: 25 (+3, +6, +3, +6,...) Solution B: 2 (+1, −2, +2, −3, +3,...) | Solution C: 120 (−5, x 3, −4, x 3, −3, ...)

Which one of the pictures in the second row logically continues the sequence in the first row?

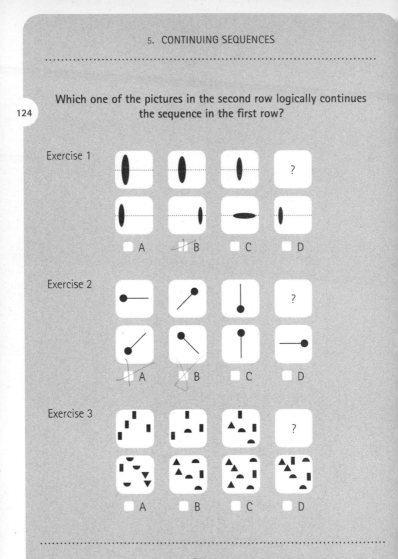

Exercise 1

☐ A   ☒ B   ☐ C   ☐ D

Exercise 2

☐ A   ☐ B   ☐ C   ☐ D

Exercise 3

☐ A   ☐ B   ☐ C   ☐ D

Solutions:

1. B (The ellipse moves from left to right, getting gradually smaller); 2. B (The baton revolves clockwise by 135 degrees each time); 3 B (In each picture a rectangle disappears. A semi-circle – then a triangle – is added. The shapes remain, however, in the same place.)

Which of the four cubes is made from the pattern?

Exercise 1

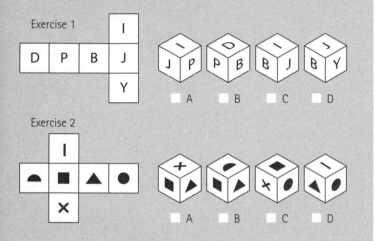

Exercise 2

Exercise 3

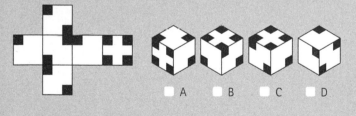

Solutions:

1. C | 2. D | 3. B

Complete the matrix with one of the six symbols given below it.
The perspective of a matrix can be vertical, horizontal, diagonal or a combination.

Exercise 1 (easy)   Exercise 2 (medium)

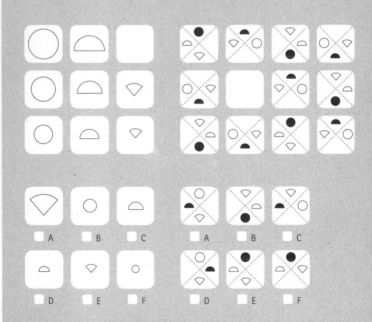

Exercise 1: The solution lies in the columns. Each column contains the same shape, which gets smaller as it goes down. Solution: A.

Exercise 2: The first solution lies in the clockwise rotation of the individual shapes in a square. In the vertical lines from left to right – in the horizontal from below to above. In addition, the circle and semi-circle are alternatively filled in and empty. Second logic: the shapes in the diagonal from left to right are always identical. Solution: E.

8. RETENTIVENESS

– Word sequences –

Take note of the following groups of words in four different categories.

🕐 2 minutes. Afterwards, turn over the page and answer a few questions.

1. Politicians:
   Obama, Eisenhower, Churchill, Bush, Nixon

2. Music genres:
   Electronica, jazz, latin, mambo, rumba

3. Internet platforms:
   Facebook, Google, Doodle, Vine, Pinterest

4. Vegetables:
   Tomato, horseradish, yams, spinach, artichoke

– Recalling a text –

Memorise the following text.

🕐 2 minutes. Turn over the page afterwards and answer a few questions.

On Friday evening, FC Basel played a match against Young Boys Bern in Basel. The home team wore their green strip and Bern played in blue. Bern unexpectedly took the lead after 15 minutes with a goal from a free kick. Those who were expecting a swift counter-attack from Basel were sorely disappointed. After half time, 28-year-old Michael Hansen, the new Basel centre forward came onto the pitch. But it was Bern who increased their lead to 2-0 with a long shot. A reckless back-pass gave Basel a fleeting hope of getting back into the game, but the 26-year-old Bern goalkeeper saved a great shot from Michael Hansen. One minute later, the unmarked Hansen struck again in front of goal but this time was given offside.

– Questions on the word sequences –

First count the sixes in this number sequence:

4562235688745228559666399696547881234564561112269699

Now answer the four following questions (do not turn back the page!)

1. Which category does the word starting with D belong to?

☐ Politicians ☐ Musical genres ☐ Internet platforms ☐ Vegetables

2. Which category does the word starting with C belong to?

☐ Politicians ☐ Musical genres ☐ Internet platforms ☐ Vegetables

3. Which category does the word starting with T belong to?

☐ Politicians ☐ Musical genres ☐ Internet platforms ☐ Vegetables

4. Which category does the word starting with H belong to?

☐ Politicians ☐ Musical genres ☐ Internet platforms ☐ Vegetables

....

– Questions on text recollection –

1. Which colour strip did the Bern team wear?

☐ Green ☐ Red ☐ Blue ☐ Yellow

2. How old was the FC Basel centre forward?

☐ 26 ☐ 27 ☐ 28 ☐ 22

3. How many goal-scoring chances did Basel have after half-time?

☐ Three ☐ Two ☐ None ☐ Four

4. How did the Bern team score a goal?

☐ Header ☐ Long shot ☐ Free kick ☐ Own goal

....

Solutions:

Number of sixes: 11. Word sequences: 1. Internet platform (Doodle) |
2. Politician (Churchill) | 3. Vegetable (Tomato) | 4. Vegetable (Horseradish)
Recalling a text: 1. blue | 2. 28 | 3. two | 4. long shot

A stone is thrown with the same force at three different angles. At which angle does the stone land on the ground the quickest?

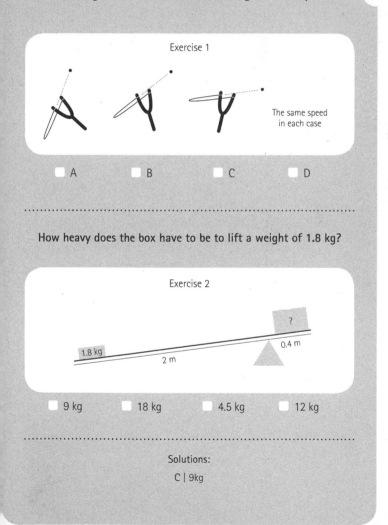

Exercise 1

The same speed in each case

☐ A   ☐ B   ☐ C   ☐ D

How heavy does the box have to be to lift a weight of 1.8 kg?

Exercise 2

1.8 kg   2 m   ?   0.4 m

☐ 9 kg   ☐ 18 kg   ☐ 4.5 kg   ☐ 12 kg

Solutions:

C | 9kg

Lifestyle & society

●—●—●—④—●

132

Am I addicted to social media?

WHAT IT'S ABOUT

On social media, we all show ourselves from our best side – and see the best side of others. We post photos of perfectly prepared meals, perfect holidays, perfect parties, and perfect children. And because of this, our online selves are far removed from our offline selves. The gap between what we're really like and how we behave on the Internet is big enough for an ocean liner to sail through. Psychologists believe that the problem lies in the perceived happiness of others that makes us doubt our own happiness. With every click, we can see our 'friends' at a party – and we're stuck at home. Our 'friends' are in a happy relationship and successful at their jobs – and we're not. Facebook makes the lonely visible.

THE TEST

A team of psychologists from the University of Essex developed a questionnaire in order to investigate this phenomenon: they call it 'FoMO' (Fear of Missing Out).

HOW IT'S EVALUATED

Forty per cent of all 35-year-olds suffer from FoMO; men more frequently than women, and adolescents more frequently than adults. If you take your child's smartphone away, even if it is only for a few hours, it's very likely that s/he will have this feeling. We know it ourselves: when we're in a bad mood or lonely, bored or stressed, we click around on Facebook. This simply reinforces our feeling of having missed out on something. It's a vicious circle.

Psychologists call it addiction when we open an app more than sixty times a day, or when we check our smartphone on waking up or just before going to sleep.

―――――― GOOD TO KNOW ――――――

Child-rearing methods in the 21st century: 'Do you want to know today's Wi-Fi password? Then clean up your rooms!'

Short FoMO test:

....

1.	I check my phone just before I go to sleep and when I wake up.	yes ☐	no ☐
2.	I have the feeling others are leading a better and more exciting life than me.	yes ☐	no ☐
3.	Even when I'm on holiday I read my emails but don't answer, so that nobody thinks I'm checking my emails while I'm away.	yes ☐	no ☐
4.	I check for updates (email, Messenger, Facebook etc.) more than four times an hour.	yes ☐	no ☐
5.	In a restaurant, I check my phone when my companion goes to the toilet.	yes ☐	no ☐
6.	I often have the feeling I've missed out when I see or hear about what others have been doing.	yes ☐	no ☐
7.	When I'm having a good time or do something exciting it's important for me to share the details online.	yes ☐	no ☐
8.	When I'm on holiday, I continue to keep tabs on what my friends are doing.	yes ☐	no ☐

....

How often did you choose "yes"?

0 to 3 times: no FoMO.
4 to 5 times: more FoMO than the average person.
6 to 8 times: heavy FoMO.

You can do the Andy Przybylskis FoMO test here: ratemyfomo.com

134

Where do I stand politically?

WHAT IT'S ABOUT

For a long time, no test was required to answer this question. Everyone knew where they stood politically: left or right. These positions originally described the seating in the French National Assembly of 1789. On the left sat the revolutionaries and on the right, the supporters of the monarchy. This word pair has defined our understanding of politics and how we talk about it ever since. When the Eastern bloc collapsed, the front page of *The Economist* asked, 'What's left?' In a dynamic, multipolar political landscape, in which the parties are vacillating more and more, and the issues they are negotiating are becoming increasingly complex, the old divisions are losing their definition.

THE TEST

Diagnostic tests can help define political orientation. One is the Political Compass™ that sounds out the political orientation of voters using a questionnaire (politicalcompass.org). In 2014, the European University Institute in Florence developed a 'Voting Advice Application' for the European elections. Your results are compared with the positions of the parties, making it possible to give voting recommendations. Here we show an excerpt from the test: euandi.eu

HOW IT'S EVALUATED

The classical left-right axis marks the economic dimension: do we prefer a strong state that steers or even regulates the economy (left)? Or should the market be self-regulating (right)? The second dimension describes living together in a society: Do we want maximum freedom in its purest form of anarchy (libertarian), or do we long for a conservative, traditional order in its most extreme form of fascism (authoritarian)?

GOOD TO KNOW

The heart beats on the left-hand side.

Put a cross next to your opinion.

....

1. There should be social benefits (unemployment benefit, social security benefits etc.) even if it means paying higher taxes.

   Agree ☐ (0)   Partly agree ☐ (2.5)   Partly disagree ☐ (7.5)   Disagree ☐ (10)

2. Foreigners should have to pay higher taxes in order to receive social benefits.

   Agree ☐ (10)   Partly agree ☐ (7.5)   Partly disagree ☐ (2.5)   Disagree ☐ (0)

3. Pensions should be cut to reduce state debts.

   Agree ☐ (10)   Partly agree ☐ (7.5)   Partly disagree ☐ (2.5)   Disagree ☐ (0)

4. State spending should be reduced to lower taxes.

   Agree ☐ (10)   Partly agree ☐ (7.5)   Partly disagree ☐ (2.5)   Disagree ☐ (0)

5. Profits from banks and stock exchange deals should be given higher tax levies.

   Agree ☐ (0)   Partly agree ☐ (2.5)   Partly disagree ☐ (7.5)   Disagree ☐ (10)

6. Employees' rights should be limited to reduce the number of unemployed.

   Agree ☐ (0)   Partly agree ☐ (2.5)   Partly disagree ☐ (7.5)   Disagree ☐ (10)

7. The state should provide better support for the unemployed.

   Agree ☐ (0)   Partly agree ☐ (2.5)   Partly disagree ☐ (7.5)   Disagree ☐ (10)

8. The state should save less in order to boost economic growth.

   Agree ☐ (0)   Partly agree ☐ (2.5)   Partly disagree ☐ (7.5)   Disagree ☐ (10)

9. Public transport should be sustained by a green tax (for example, tolls).

   Agree ☐ (0/10) Partly agree ☐ (2.5/7.5) Partly disagree ☐ (7.5/2.5) Disagree ☐ (10/0)

10. Renewable energy should be supported by the state even if this leads to higher energy costs for the population.

    Agree ☐ (0/10) Partly agree ☐ (2.5/7.5) Partly disagree ☐ (7.5/2.5) Disagree ☐ (10/0)

11. Immigration should be dealt with more restrictively.

    Agree ☐ (0) Partly agree ☐ (2.5) Partly disagree ☐ (7.5) Disagree ☐ (10)

12. Immigrants should adopt the predominant culture and its traditional values.

    Agree ☐ (0) Partly agree ☐ (2.5) Partly disagree ☐ (7.5) Disagree ☐ (10)

13. You are in favour of same-sex marriage.

    Agree ☐ (10) Partly agree ☐ (7.5) Partly disagree ☐ (2.5) Disagree ☐ (0)

14. Embryonal stem cell research should be stopped.

    Agree ☐ (0) Partly agree ☐ (2.5) Partly disagree ☐ (7.5) Disagree ☐ (10)

15. You are in favour of active euthanasia.

    Agree ☐ (10) Partly agree ☐ (7.5) Partly disagree ☐ (2.5) Disagree ☐ (0)

16. The limitation of personal privacy on the Internet has to be accepted for the sake of public security.

    Agree ☐ (0) Partly agree ☐ (2.5) Partly disagree ☐ (7.5) Disagree ☐ (10)

17. Criminals should be punished more severely.

    Agree ☐ (0) Partly agree ☐ (2.5) Partly disagree ☐ (7.5) Disagree ☐ (10)

18. Abortion should be restricted.

    Agree ☐ (0) Partly agree ☐ (2.5) Partly disagree ☐ (7.5) Disagree ☐ (10)

1. Add up the points you gave to questions 1-10 (the first number each time for questions 9 and 10) and mark the total on the LEFT-RIGHT axis with a cross.

2. Add up the points you gave to questions 9-18 (the second number each time for questions 9 and 10) and mark the total on the CONSERVATIVE-LIBERAL axis with a cross.

3. Draw a vertical line through the cross on the LEFT-RIGHT axis and a horizontal line through the cross on the CONSERVATIVE-LIBERAL axis. The intersection of the two lines shows where you stand politically.

4. Ask yourself: Where did I stand ten years ago?

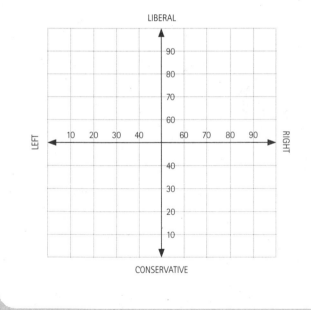

The questionnaire was reprinted (in an abbreviated and adapted form) with the kind permission of the European University Institute in Florence, Professor Alexander Trechsel.

How sexist am I?

WHAT IT'S ABOUT

Culture experts like to point out that our pop-culture consumer society reflects our social structures and preferences. This means that the popularity of certain feature films, for example, tells us how sexist a society is: and more importantly, how sexist you are.

THE TEST

Think of your favourite film, one that you've watched many times. Can you picture it? Ask yourself the following three questions: Is there more than one woman in the film whose name we are told? Do the women talk to each other? Do the women talk to each other about anything other than men?

HOW IT'S EVALUATED

If you can't answer all three questions with 'yes', then the film is androcentric, or centred on men. The Bechdel test, named after a comic strip by American cartoonist Alison Bechdel, uses these questions to test whether women play independent roles in a film. And it allows conclusions to be made about our everyday lives: it seems that we prefer films in which women are merely accessories to men.

Musicals and horror films, incidentally, are the most women-friendly genres whereas only 25 per cent of Westerns and 30 per cent of all war films pass the test. On average, female characters are younger than males. Women are most often shown cooking, cleaning, talking and having sex. Men are usually shown in job scenarios and violent situations.

In Swedish cinemas, films that pass the test are now marked on the poster (with an A rating), which indicates that things are changing. And the Representation Project by Jennifer Seibel Newsom and Regina K. Scully takes things a step further: their test examines not only gender but also the age, sexual orientation, weight and ethnicity of actresses.

GOOD TO KNOW

'Don't call a woman a bitch. Call her an asshole. It still gets your point across and it's not sexist'. *Eleanor Roosevelt*

Which film directors do you like?

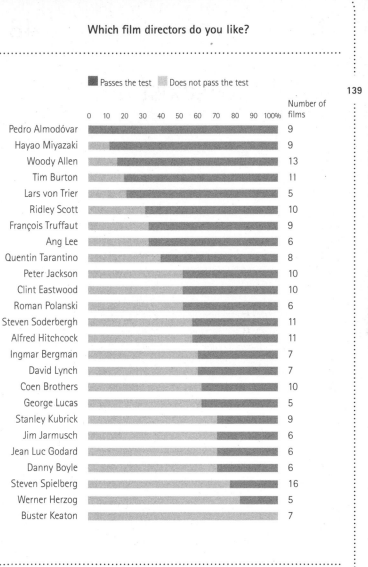

Passes the test · Does not pass the test

Director	Number of films
Pedro Almodóvar	9
Hayao Miyazaki	9
Woody Allen	13
Tim Burton	11
Lars von Trier	5
Ridley Scott	10
François Truffaut	9
Ang Lee	6
Quentin Tarantino	8
Peter Jackson	10
Clint Eastwood	10
Roman Polanski	6
Steven Soderbergh	11
Alfred Hitchcock	11
Ingmar Bergman	7
David Lynch	7
Coen Brothers	10
George Lucas	5
Stanley Kubrick	9
Jim Jarmusch	6
Jean Luc Godard	6
Danny Boyle	6
Steven Spielberg	16
Werner Herzog	5
Buster Keaton	7

This is a shortened version of Daniel Mariani's information diagram, 'Visualisation of the Bechdel Test'.

www.tenchocolatesundaes.blogspot.com.br

Am I a perpetrator or a victim?

WHAT IT'S ABOUT

Many people don't know that they have prejudices. This is the conclusion of probably the most famous discrimination test, the Implicit Association Test, or IAT. It measures the discrepancy between our conscious convictions and subconscious prejudices.

THE TEST

First, you are asked about your attitudes. Most people will say, 'I like black and white people equally.' Next, you are asked in quick succession to assign positive and negative attributes to people in photographs with different skin colours. The test measures our spontaneous associations when not influenced by reflection. On the implicit.harvard.edu website you can carry out the test yourself. You will find tests there on varying forms of discrimination – skin colour, gender, weight, age, and also country-specific tests.

HOW IT'S EVALUATED

Seventy per cent of us have a subconscious 'preference for whites', which means that it takes significantly longer to associate positive words with dark skin colour. But how can you influence your subconscious? If, directly before doing the test, you look at photographs of dark-skinned people that have positive connotations, such as Martin Luther King, you will also associate the test photos with more positive characteristics. We are what we see.

One question does not come up in the test: Who is discriminated against? Rudolfo Mendoza-Denton from Columbia University is one of the few researchers who puts the position of those stigmatised in the foreground. The page opposite gives you an impression of his work.

--- GOOD TO KNOW ---

'In the end, we will remember not the words of our enemies but the silence of our friends'. *Martin Luther King Jr.*

Evaluate the following statements on a scale of 1–5.

very unconcerned 1 2 3 4 5 very concerned

1. Imagine you are sitting on a bus. The bus is full except for two seats, one of which is the seat next to you. As the bus comes to a stop, a woman gets in. How concerned/anxious would you be that she might avoid sitting next to you because of your race/ethnicity?

   1 2 3 4 5

2. Imagine you're driving down the street, and there is a police barricade just ahead. The police officers are randomly pulling people over to check drivers' licences and registrations. How concerned/anxious would you be that an officer might pull you over because of your race/ethnicity?

   1 2 3 4 5

3. Imagine that you are standing in line for the ATM machine, and you notice the woman at the machine glances back while she's getting her money. How concerned/anxious would you be that she might be suspicious of you because of your race/ethnicity?

   1 2 3 4 5

< 5 points: You do not know the feeling of being stigmatised due to your skin colour or ethnicity. Ask yourself: If I reverse the situations – in other words, as a passenger on a bus, as a policeman/woman doing a traffic check, or getting money from an ATM – how do I react to people of other ethnicity?

> 6 points: You know the feeling of being stigmatised. Ask yourself: Do I have a strategy to cope with discriminating situations?

☛ The entire questionnaire and study can be read on the institute's website: socialrelations.psych.columbia.edu.

With the kind permission of the Social Relations Laboratory, Columbia University

142

Am I rich?

WHAT IT'S ABOUT

One question that we perpetually ask ourselves is: 'When can I consider myself rich?' A millionaire is rich, for example, but a million is not nearly as much as it used to be. Other definitions gauge wealth in relation to the average national income: in the EU, for example, you are considered rich if you earn more than twice the average net income of your country. In Germany, this would apply to all people with an annual income of approximately 60,000 euros. Another interpretation defines all those who can live off their interest as rich. 'Ultra High Net Worth Individuals' are people with assets of more then 30 million dollars; the 'super-rich' label applies to those with 300 million dollars upwards. During the wave of Occupy protests, there was much talk of the 'one per cent' – the richest one per cent of people whose fortune is 65 times bigger than the poorer half of the world population. But who exactly is this one per cent? Will you ever belong to this group? On the right-hand side, you can find out.

THE TEST

The sociologists Glenn Firebaugh and Laura M. Tach asked people to choose between two scenarios:
A: You earn 60,000 dollars a year, and your colleagues earn 50,000.
B: You earn 80,000 dollars a year, and your colleagues earn 90,000.
What would you choose?

HOW IT'S EVALUATED

The majority of people chose option A. They would sacrifice 20,000 dollars a year just to earn more than their colleagues. This shows that we define wealth in relation to our environment. In other words, money only makes you happy when you have more than your neighbour. Which is why a millionaire could feel poor in the company of a multi-millionaire!

GOOD TO KNOW

'He who has less than he desires should know that he has more than he's worth.'
Georg Christoph Lichtenberg

How much do you earn per year?

From 27,000 euros upwards, you belong to the 'one per cent'.

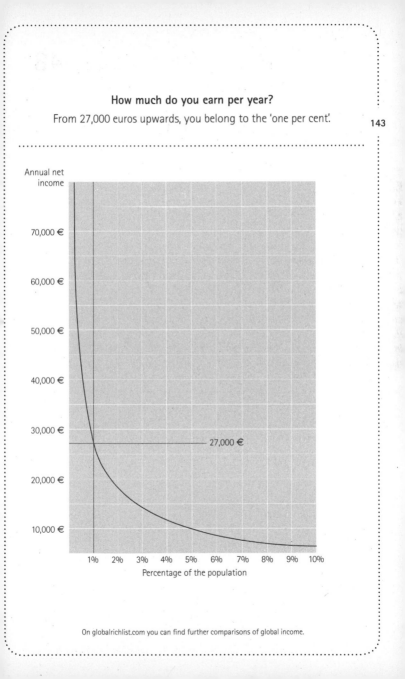

On globalrichlist.com you can find further comparisons of global income.

144

When will I die?

WHAT IT'S ABOUT

One thing is certain: we're all going to die. The only question is: when? There is in fact a statistical answer to this question. Using so-called 'death tables', insurance actuaries can calculate when their clients are likely to die. Death tables are nothing new: In ancient Rome, an official called Domitius Ulpianus was in charge of the Praetorians' taxation system. His assumption that a 40-year-old would live for another twenty years, and a sixty-year-old only five, resulted in high tax levies for many Praetorians. The legend goes that these people took revenge on Ulpianus and killed him without further ado.

THE TEST

The death table is not really a test; it's a calculation. Put simply, the likelihood of death is calculated in the following way: the number of deaths at a given age divided by the number of people who have reached this age. Current death tables presently stop at 130 years old, upwards of which the likelihood of death stands at 100 per cent.

HOW IT'S EVALUATED

You can find out from the table how old you may become. The older you get, the more your life expectancy increases. It is well known that women live a few years longer than men. This data is applicable to Germany. In Switzerland, you can add roughly two years and in Austria, a few months.

GOOD TO KNOW

These factors influence how old you will become:
1. Genetic disposition (Did your parents live to be older than 80?)
2. Social status (Do you have a university degree? Do you earn above the average?)
3. Lifestyle (Are you overweight? Do you smoke? Do you do sport?
Do you have a family?)

The death table: how many years do I have left to live?

My age ♂	How many years I have left to live	My age ♀	How many years I have left to live
1	77.0	1	82.0
10	68.1	10	73.1
20	58.3	20	63.2
25	53.4	25	58.2
27	51.5	27	56.2
29	49.5	29	54.3
31	47.6	31	52.3
33	45.7	33	50.3
35	43.7	35	48.4
37	41.8	37	46.4
39	39.9	39	44.5
41	38.0	41	42.5
43	36.1	43	40.6
45	34.2	45	38.7
47	32.4	47	36.8
49	30.6	49	34.9
51	28.8	51	33.1
53	27.1	53	31.2
55	25.4	55	29.4
60	21.3	60	25.0
65	17.5	65	20.7
70	13.9	70	16.5
80	7.8	80	9.1
90	3.8	90	4.3
100	2.0	100	2.1

Am I happy?

WHAT IT'S ABOUT

What is happiness? And how can I find it? Most researchers agree that the situation we are born into – our biological disposition – social and cultural expectations, unplanned events and our own behaviour are the factors that most influence our feelings of happiness. That would be one answer to the question of how you find happiness. What remains, however, is the question that causes disputes among researchers: What is happiness? And more precisely, how do you measure it? There is no thermometer and there are no indicators. Even brainwave measurements do not produce reliable results. People with healthy children, stable marriages, successful careers and their own homes would be described as happy in the USA, for example. Nevertheless, such people can be absolutely miserable.

If we aren't living on the breadline, our feeling of happiness can only be determined to a certain degree by external factors. We are the only ones who can describe ourselves as happy or unhappy. Or, as the Roman poet Publilius Syrus, declared: 'Happy is not he who seems happy to others but he who thinks himself lucky'.

THE TEST

Even if there are different cultural definitions of happiness, nearly everyone has a feeling for whether they are happy or not, says US psychologist Sonja Lyubomirsky. She has developed a questionnaire that examines subjective personal happiness using four questions – see the right-hand page.

GOOD TO KNOW

What you can do yourself:
1. Cultivate friendships even when you feel bad. Happiness is the only thing you can give without having it yourself. 2. Change perspective. Every evening, jot down two good things that happened during the day. 3. Do things. The opposite of happiness is not unhappiness but boredom.

For each of the following statements and/or questions, circle the point on the scale that you feel is most appropriate in describing you.

1. In general, I consider myself:

not a very happy person   ① — ② — ③ — ④ — ⑤ — ⑥ — ⑦   a very happy person

2. Compared to most of my peers, I consider myself:

less happy   ① — ② — ③ — ④ — ⑤ — ⑥ — ⑦   more happy

3. Some people are generally very happy. They enjoy life regardless of what is going on, getting the most out of everything. To what extent does this characterisation describe you?

not at all   ① — ② — ③ — ④ — ⑤ — ⑥ — ⑦   a great deal

4. Some people are generally not very happy. Although they are not depressed, they never seem as happy as they might be. To what extent does this characterisation describe you?

not at all   ① — ② — ③ — ④ — ⑤ — ⑥ — ⑦   a great deal

Count up your points and divide by four.

⚠ Question four is inverted: a1 is a7 and vice versa, 2 is 6 and vice versa, 3 is 5 and vice versa, 4 stays 4. Compare yourself to the norm groups.

	16% of people questioned	Average	16% of people questioned
Russian adult	< 3.09	4.02	> 4.95
American adult	< 4.66	5.62	> 6.58
Russian teenager	< 3.71	4.84	> 5.97
American teenager	< 3.78	4.89	> 6.00

Subjective Happiness Scale and norm comparisons with the kind permission of Sonja Lyubomirsky.

Is it love?

WHAT IT'S ABOUT

'The imperative that couples should keep up the tension in their relationship is one of the more absurd imperatives of our times.' This is the beginning of Dutch writer Connie Palmen's short description of the nature of love. She gets to grips with the fairly important question: Why is tension needed to hold a relationship together? As a guarantee for good sex? Because we live as if we were acting in a TV series and want to be pumped up by intrigues and lies all the time?

To be precise, Palmen continues, only the start of a relationship is fraught with tension. At the start, we are insecure. At the start, we're afraid of being abandoned. At the start, we're afraid that our partner might discover our weaknesses and faults. The first years of a relationship are the ones in which we learn to put aside our insecurities and accept each other's faults. We reduce tension. If tension persists, the relationship fails. If a relationship needs tension at all costs, it's already in its death throes. A relationship should not be artificially inflated with tension, writes Palmen, because constant tension is inherent to relationships anyway, due to the fear that one day, things will change. Palmen's partner died of cancer.

THE TEST

This definition of love is unusual. There are many others and none of them are 'right'. There is no reliable test, therefore, to find out whether what we feel is love. So we have based our test not on the parascientific matchmaking of dating agencies but on four clever questions that a Norwegian priest from Bergen asks couples before they get married.

GOOD TO KNOW

'Do not hide in love from things of time / Nor in things of time from love.'
Erich Fried

Take a quiet moment to ask yourself the following questions:

1. Do I like myself in the company of my partner?

2. Can I imagine my partner as the parent of my children?

3. Do we both prefer to sleep with the window open or closed?

4. Would I take myself in my arms if I woke up next to myself?

1. Whether we feel good in the company of another is decisive in whether we enjoy being with that person or not.

2. This question tries to sound out the long-term potential of this spontaneous love.

3. Relationships are routines, routines are habits and habits are the fingerprints of character.

4. 'Love is never in the one who is loved but in the one who loves. We cannot find the love missing in ourselves in others', writes German social psychologist Erich Fromm.

150

How good is my sex life?

We will hail back to the classic of sex tests, the Index of Sexual Satisfaction (ISS). It was developed in 1992 by Walter W. Hudson and does not so much measure the sexual satisfaction in a couple's relationship but rather whether there are disorders. The original questionnaire contained 25 questions, and has proved itself to be reliable in scientific tests. To warm up, we ask 11 of these questions and simplify the evaluation: to get a first impression, answer every question with either yes (I agree with the statement) or no (I don't agree with the statement). And consider how your partner would answer.

--- GOOD TO KNOW ---

'I don't understand the question but sex is probably the answer.' *Woody Allen*

1. I feel that my partner enjoys our sex life.
   yes ☐ (0)　　　no ☐ (1)

2. Sex is fun for my partner and me.
   yes ☐ (0)　　　no ☐ (1)

3. Our sex life is monotonous.
   yes ☐ (1)　　　no ☐ (0)

4. I feel that my partner wants too much sex from me.
   yes ☐ (1)　　　no ☐ (0)

5. I try to avoid sexual contact with my partner.

   yes ☐ (1)   no ☐ (0)

6. My partner does not want sex when I do.

   yes ☐ (1)   no ☐ (0)

7. I feel that our sex life really adds a lot to our relationship.

   yes ☐ (0)   no ☐ (1)

8. My partner seems to avoid sexual contact with me.

   yes ☐ (1)   no ☐ (0)

9. It is easy for me to get sexually excited by my partner.

   yes ☐ (0)   no ☐ (1)

10. I feel that my partner is sexually pleased with me.

   yes ☐ (0)   no ☐ (1)

11. My partner does not satisfy me sexually.

   yes ☐ (1)   no ☐ (0)

....

Add up your score in each of the check boxes.

Total: ☐

< 4 points = Your sex life seems to be fine.

≥ 4 points = Your score points to disorders. If you feel that this is causing
              problems, you should consider answering the full ISS questionnaire
              and seek advice.

....

With the kind permission of Myrna Hudson, Walmyr Publishing Company.

152

How well do I know my partner?

'Did you say something?' 'No, that was yesterday'. This joke, written by Robert Gernhardt for comedian Otto Waalkes, describes the point when couples stop talking to one another. Before it gets to this point, here is a short questionnaire to test how up to date your knowledge of one another is.

───────── GOOD TO KNOW ─────────

'Hope is the last thing to die. If it had died sooner, there wouldn't be so many disappointed people.' *Werner Butter*

⚠ **Your partner asks you the following 14 questions.**

You answer and your partner decides whether the answer was right or wrong.

1. Which two subjects have been on my mind most recently?   right ☐   wrong ☐

2. Which of my relatives annoys me the most?   right ☐   wrong ☐

3. What's my attitude towards religion?   right ☐   wrong ☐

4. As a child, what did I want to be when I grew up?   right ☐   wrong ☐

5. Who do I talk to when I have relationship problems? right ☐ wrong ☐

6. Which two people have bothered me recently? right ☐ wrong ☐

7. What drink do I order in my local bar? right ☐ wrong ☐

8. What book am I reading at the moment, or what did I read last? right ☐ wrong ☐

9. What was the name of my last partner before you? right ☐ wrong ☐

10. What is/was my mother's maiden name? right ☐ wrong ☐

11. How much do I earn per month? right ☐ wrong ☐

12. When did we last have sex? right ☐ wrong ☐

13. Which of our friends could I most imagine being together with? right ☐ wrong ☐

14. Where would I like to live? right ☐ wrong ☐

....

There is one point per right answer.

Total points: ☐

> 11 points: Unbelievable!
Ask yourself whether you check up too much on your partner.

7–11 points: You know a great deal.
Ask yourself what you would like to know about your partner.

< 7 points: Congratulations!
You give your partner breathing space.

Am I a good mother or father?

WHAT IT'S ABOUT

Modern parents can be many things – such as helicopter or curling parents. 'Helicopter parenting' is a term used to describe parents who never let their children out of their sight, mostly in order to achieve two things: security and later job success. In Sweden, these kinds of parents are called *Curlingföräldrar*, because the parents tirelessly remove obstacles from their children's path like the sweepers in curling. The all-important aspect of this kind of parent is not whether the child will go on to have a career but that s/he will be able to say: I had a happy childhood.

THE TEST

There are a series of parents' tests. Only a few are serious, and some of them are hilarious. Colin Bowles, for example, the author of *The Beginner's Guide to Fatherhood* tries to help you find out whether or not you are ready for children in the first place. This is how you simulate being a parent: Repeat everything you say at least five times. Carry a wet, four-to-six kilo sack around from 5 to 10 pm while your mobile phone rings incessantly. At 10 pm, put the sack down. Pick it back up again at 11 pm and carry it around again until 1 am. Set your alarm clock to 3 am. Since you can't fall asleep, get up again at 2 am. Lie back down at 2.45. At 3 am, your alarm clock rings. Sing lullabies in the dark until 4 am. Get up at 5 am and make breakfast.

HOW IT'S EVALUATED

If you can do all this for five whole years and still act cheerfully, happily, and as if you had a good night's sleep, then you are ready for children.

--- GOOD TO KNOW ---

Parent quick-check: What do you do differently from your parents? What do you do in exactly the same way?

Ask your children.

Either you can put yourself through complex psychological tests, such as the 'Parenting Stress Index' (PSI) or you can simply ask your children:

1. What would you prefer: more pocket money or more time with me?

2. What am I like when I'm angry?

3. How should I punish you when you do something that's not allowed?

4. What am I like when I'm in a good mood?

5. What's the best reward you can possibly imagine?

6. What do you like doing with me?

7. What would you like to do if we had a lot of time?

8. And the last question is directed at you again: What would you like to do with your child if you had a lot of time?

An evaluation is not necessary here – your children's answers will speak for themselves.

How German am I?

If you're young and a writer, film-maker, or designer, if you have a beard and speak English, you will sooner or later end up in Berlin. Berlin is the capital of hipsters. But it's also the capital of Germany. And one question that everyone who has moved there from abroad asks is: How German am I?

Adam Fletcher, a British writer, has written a clever book on becoming German that is based on this test. It is thoroughly tongue-in-cheek. But that's not to say it's all wrong. Tick the appropriate answers!

─────── GOOD TO KNOW ───────

Two Martinis, *bitte*. Dry? *Nein*, I said TWO!

1. You are at my house and very *durstig*. I place a glass of liquid in front of you. You observe it closely and notice it does not appear to be fizzing. What do you do?

   A ☐ Why would a liquid need to fizz?
   B ☐ Say 'I'm sorry but my *Schorle* appears to be *kaputt*'.
   C ☐ Drink it, but make a mental note to de-friend me.

2. Someone voices an opinion you do not agree with, how are you most likely to respond?

   A ☐ *Das macht keinen Sinn.*
   B ☐ Your opinion is interesting, here is mine.
   C ☐ *Total unlogisch!*

2. What name is your Facebook account under?

   A ☐ Your real name.
   B ☐ Your name, but divided in some way like 'An Tje'.
   C ☐ *Hallo?!* Prism is not just a shape you know. Wake up people!

4. **A female friend has purchased a new skirt, she models it for you, you don't like it very much, what do you say?**

   A ☐ It's nice. How much did it cost?

   B ☐ *Nein. Bitte nicht.*

   C ☐ A skirt? Totally impractical.

5. **Whilst casually discussing the movie *Slumdog Millionaire*, your conversation partner mistakenly states the movie's release date as 2007, when you know for a fact that it was 2009. What do you do?**

   A ☐ Nothing. It was just a simple mistake.

   B ☐ Silently turn and walk away. This conversation is over!

   C ☐ *Klugscheiß* them. Say 'I think you'll find the movie was released in 2009. If I'm not mistaken on the 19th March. *Oder?*'

6. **You are meeting a male friend for the third time, you consider your relationship to be '*ziemlich gut*'. How do you greet each other?**

   A ☐ The handshake

   B ☐ The hug

   C ☐ The hugshake, an indecisive combination of both the handshake and the hug, beginning first with the handshake, then changing your mind mid-shake, morphing the greeting into a stiff hug that squishes the shaking hands in between you.

. . . .

Add up your points:

A = 1 point, B = 2 points, C = 3 points

< 12 points

Schade. You're officially less German than the average. *Kipp* all your windows, pour yourself an *Apfelsaftschorle*, practice your *klugscheißing* and there might still be some hope for you yet.

>12 *Punkte*

Nicht so schlecht! You're officially more German than the average. You're as German as *Pfand* and shouting at people who commit minor legal infractions like crossing the road on a red *Ampelmännchen*.

. . . .

With the kind permission of Adam Fletcher

Knowledge
& beliefs

160

Am I a smart-ass?

☛ First, please do the test on the right-hand page.

WHAT IT'S ABOUT
Do you have a broad general knowledge, and don't hesitate to point out other people's errors? Do you think you know everything and everyone? Then this test should bring you back down to earth.

THE TEST
The familiarity test (right-hand page) does not check how many celebrities you know. It's a test to find out how strongly you veer towards talking about things you know nothing about. And in this case, how often you claim to know someone that doesn't even exist. Now do the test.

HOW IT'S EVALUATED
Did you give Frank T. Elliott, Anton Kronenberg, Thomas Flury or Francis Delacroix one or even two points? Well, these people don't even exist!

The OCQ (Over-Claiming Questionnaire) is an ingeniously simple instrument conceived by psychology professor Delroy Paulhus to expose smart-asses.

Did you pass the test with flying colours? Well done! But that doesn't mean you aren't a fib-teller. Our potential to 'over-claim', according to Paulhus, depends on the situation. In a conversation with a potential employer or possible love interest, we are more likely to put ourselves in a good light. 'Social desirability' describes the impulse to want to fulfil the expectations of your counterpart. We all know the feeling of 'over-claiming': in a nice group of people, with stimulating conversation, a couple of book titles or names of bands are passed around that we've never heard before. And because we don't want to out ourselves as being clueless, we pretend to know them.

--- GOOD TO KNOW ---

Just ask if you don't know something.

How well informed are you?

Evaluate these public figures according to the following criteria:
2 = I've definitely heard of him/her 1= I might have heard of him/her
0= I definitely haven't heard of him/her

1. ☐ Nelson Mandela
2. ☐ Miley Cyrus
3. ☐ Wendy Cope
4. ☐ Anthony Grey
5. ☐ Thomas Flury
6. ☐ Jansher Khan
7. ☐ David Beckham
8. ☐ Dietrich Mateschitz
9. ☐ Geoffrey Boycott
10. ☐ Robert Crumb
11. ☐ Frank T. Elliott
12. ☐ Anton Kronenberg
13. ☐ Beryl Bainbridge
14. ☐ Miquita Oliver
15. ☐ Francis Delacroix

Add up the points that you gave to persons no. 5, 11, 12, and 15:

☞ You will find the evaluation on the left-hand page.

Simplified version of the Over-Claiming Questionnaire, with the kind permission of the authors.

162

Will I crack the million jackpot?

The TV series 'Who Wants To Be A Millionaire' unites two of the greatest needs of the 21st century: knowledegability and earning a fast buck. In Germany, at the time this book went to print, eight candidates in total had managed to crack the million-euro jackpot. Here are eight of the finalists' questions:

--- GOOD TO KNOW ---

If you need a 'lifeline', the authors of this book are more than willing to help:
+41 76 3032292

Who was standing at the top of Mount Everest with Edmund Hillary in 1953?

A Nasreddin Hodscha ☐   B Nursay Pimsorn ☐

C Tenzing Norgay ☐   D Abrindranath Singh ☐

1

In the pop group The Bee Gees, which of the two Gibb brothers are twins?

A Robin and Barry ☐   B Maurice and Robin ☐

C Barry and Maurice ☐   D Andy and Robin ☐

2

Which writer, in his capacity as an architect, built an open-air swimming pool in Zurich?

A Joseph Roth ☐   B Martin Walser ☐

C Max Frisch ☐   D Friedrich Dürrenmatt ☐

3

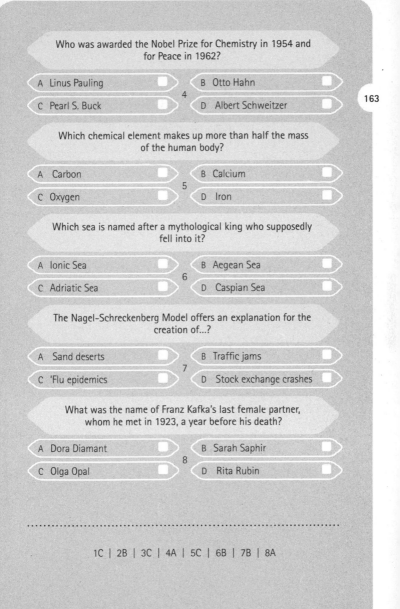

Who was awarded the Nobel Prize for Chemistry in 1954 and for Peace in 1962?

A Linus Pauling

B Otto Hahn

C Pearl S. Buck

D Albert Schweitzer

4

Which chemical element makes up more than half the mass of the human body?

A Carbon

B Calcium

C Oxygen

D Iron

5

Which sea is named after a mythological king who supposedly fell into it?

A Ionic Sea

B Aegean Sea

C Adriatic Sea

D Caspian Sea

6

The Nagel-Schreckenberg Model offers an explanation for the creation of...?

A Sand deserts

B Traffic jams

C 'Flu epidemics

D Stock exchange crashes

7

What was the name of Franz Kafka's last female partner, whom he met in 1923, a year before his death?

A Dora Diamant

B Sarah Saphir

C Olga Opal

D Rita Rubin

8

1C | 2B | 3C | 4A | 5C | 6B | 7B | 8A

Do I have a clever child?

WHAT IT'S ABOUT

No one would dispute that reading, writing and maths are skills in life that are useful rather than hindrances. But aptitude tests in education have changed direction in a way that was probably unintentional. Education today prepares children for the next test rather than preparing them for life. 'Teaching to the test' is the name for this in the USA. Even the famous PISA tests (Programme for International Student Assessment) do not measure the capabilities that make us wonderful human beings, but simply the capabilities that are required to pass the PISA tests.

THE TEST

Jane has cycled to a river from home, a distance of 4km. The journey took her 9 minutes. On the way home, she took a shorter route of 3km. This only took her 6 minutes. What is Jane's average speed on the way to the river and on the way back?

This is the format for a typical ninth-grade PISA test in mathematics. But who is capable of solving this kind of puzzle? Aside from PISA, many countries have introduced their own national torture instruments such as SAT, the college entrance exams in the USA, the 11+ grammar school test in England or the 'Gymi-Test' in Switzerland – the equivalent of waterboarding among standard tests. A small comfort for parents who already strive from the moment their children enter first grade to ensure that they get into grammar school: in 1930, the comprehensive education of primary school children was still considered to be 'very good' if they could answer questions such as those on the right. This knowledge test appeared in 1930 in the November issue of the US *Parent's Magazine*.

--------- GOOD TO KNOW ---------

This is the best way you can cheat in an exam: Carefully peel the label off a plastic bottle and write formulas or key words on the back of the label. Stick it back on. If you are completely stuck in the exam, look deep into the bottle.

What 7 to 10-year-olds needed to know in 1930.

1. Are all apples red?

2. In what season do green leaves change colour?

3. Does the Atlantic Ocean consist of fire, water, paper or earth?

4. How many cents are there in a euro? (Original question: How many nickels are there in a quarter?)

5. Does ice melt in the sun?

6. If you sit in a car, do cars coming your way drive past your left or your right? (NB: original test is American)

7. Do fish have feathers?

8. If elderly people enter the room, is it more polite to

   a) remain seated?
   b) get up and leave without saying anything?
   c) get up and only sit back down when the elderly person has sat down or has left the room?

9. What is heavier: a pound of potatoes or a pound of sugar?

1. No | 2. Autumn | 3. Water | 4. 100 | 5. Yes | 6. Left | 7. No | 8. c) | 9. Both weigh the same.

☛ Jane's average speed along the entire route is: 4 + 3 = 7 km in 9 + 6 = 15 minutes = 1/4 hour; 7 x 4 = 28 km/h.

More than five correct answers = good
More than seven correct answers = extraordinarily high
All correct = almost impossible

166

Am I clever?

WHAT IT'S ABOUT

Because dealing with the unknown is considered one of the key competences of academic thinking, Oxbridge interviews often include a brainteaser – an apparently absurd question to which there is sometimes a correct answer (see right) but whose actual purpose is to give the interviewers an insight into how you think. Here is a brief example:

THE TEST

Let's say you were asked: How many inhabitants does Brooklyn have? No idea? Let's go through it together step by step. New York is a city with approximately 8 or 9 million inhabitants. How many districts does it have? The Beastie Boys wrote a tribute to New York with their album *To the 5 Boroughs*. We know four of them: Manhattan, Queens, Brooklyn, Bronx – but what was the fifth district called again? If, for the sake of simplicity, we presume that districts we have named are equally large but the fifth is smaller because it is unknown, then divide the approximately 9 million inhabitants by 4.5. That makes 2 million. Not bad, Brooklyn has 2.5 million inhabitants! The entrance committee is not interested whether you actually know the number of inhabitants in Brooklyn but whether you can use deduction as a strategy for problem-solving.

John Farndon has collected this and other puzzles in his enjoyable book *Do You Think You're Clever?*, including that very question itself. One of the best questions is 'How many animals did Noah take onto the ark?' or 'Why are the words "God" and "I" written in capital letters in English?' And only for advanced students: 'I think *Hamlet* is too long, don't you?' The mother of all brainteasers, however, has to be 'Is this a question?'

GOOD TO KNOW

It's helpful to imagine that you're sitting with friends in the pub while being in this interview. No one is going to be impressed by your knowledge, but everyone is going to be impressed by your way of thinking. Examiners, after all are only human.

You have a three-litre container and a five-litre container. Measure off four litres.

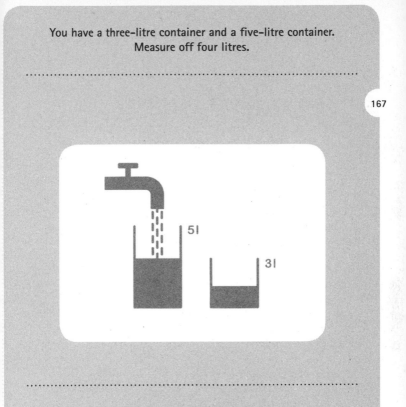

This is a well-known problem from the film *Die Hard III*, when its two heroes have to solve the puzzle to stop a bomb from exploding. The solution: fill the five-litre container with water and from this container pour three litres into the other container. Then two litres are left in the larger container. Now empty the smaller container and pour the remaining two litres from the larger container. Then fill the larger container again and pour the water into the smaller container until it is full. As it contained two litres of water beforehand, there is still space for exactly one litre. In the larger container, five minus one litre remains, making four litres.

168.

Am I talking to a robot?

WHAT IT'S ABOUT

In the film *Blade Runner*, robots don't just look like people; they behave like them too. Only a highly complex psychometric procedure, the Voigt-Kampff Test, can distinguish between man and machine. The dividing line, as we'll see, is drawn along empathy: people are capable of showing empathy whereas machines are not.

This 'replicant' test features in the book by Philip K. Dick on which the film was based, and is inspired by the work of British logician Alan Turing. As early as 1950, he had asked the simple yet far-sighted question: 'Can machines think?'

THE TEST

Turing's experimental set-up – the Turing Test – works like this: you interrogate two partners that you can neither see nor hear. One partner is a person; the other is a computer. Both try to convince you that they are human. Your task is to find out which one is which. If you are still unable to establish this after a long exchange, the machine has won. And although computers

these days are becoming ever more sophisticated – and 'human' – (for example to outwit people, software has been devised that makes spelling mistakes, tries to impress with cool one-liners, or is generally sceptical or grumpy), only one chatbot in history has succeeded in hoodwinking people. The Eugene Goostman computer, programmed by Russian developers, was thought to be a 13-year-old Ukrainian boy by 33 per cent of the judges at a Turing event in London.

HOW IT'S EVALUATED

Alan Turing predicted that by the year 2000, computers would exist that would only be identified as machines after a five-minute conversation with a human interrogator 70 per cent of the time. That his prophecy has only been fulfilled once since then is considered by some as proof of the complexity of human intelligence. Others regard it as proof that the Turing Test has become outdated.

Whether the test is nonsense or not, the more interesting question is: What question would you ask a computer in order to find out whether it's a machine? Because that says a lot about how we regard machines. Those who ask general knowledge questions as though they are playing Trivial Pursuit, (e.g. 'What's the capital city of Angola?' In which year was the UN founded?) do not stand a chance, of course. Any common-or-garden search engine can answer these kinds of questions. In times of Wikipedia and Google, this kind of knowledge actually points more to a machine – no human learns these kinds of answers off by heart any more.

One clever way in which machines can be found out is by asking them personal questions. A few years ago, in answer to the question 'Who created you?', a test robot answered: 'The programming language AIML'. But the most tricky area for machines is common sense – the fundamental human capacity to see through banalities and nonsense in a flash. 'Can giraffes drive cars?' Even

a child knows that they can't. But if you Google the question, you will find an astonishing number of hits for giraffes spotted on motorways, or EU regulations for animal transport. A computer will answer the question incorrectly because no one will ever have bothered to enter the correct answer in a database. So we come to the paradoxical conclusion that, when it comes to machines: the easier it is, the trickier.

The most secure methods of exposing machines are so-called Winograd Schemata. These are banal questions that become unintelligible for computers through grammatical tricks. An example is 'Question: The large ball crashed right through the table because it was made of Styrofoam. What was made of Styrofoam? The ball or the table?' This kind of question requires common sense (which computers don't have) and the capacity to interpret the grammatical reference (which computers cannot do).

How are you?

--------- GOOD TO KNOW ---------

If you surf the Internet, you continually come across little Turing tests: commands to type blurred and distorted rows of letters. These CAPTCHA tests, whose name derives from the Turing Test (Completely Automated Public Turing Test to Tell Computers and Humans Apart), are puzzles that only a human can solve.

170

Am I ready?

WHAT IT'S ABOUT

In many religions, life is seen as a test. Those who pass it enter paradise (→ Afterlife Test, p. 172). In Zen, there is neither heaven nor hell, only 'being'. As being is fraught with illusions, Zen monks developed a tool to break through these illusions: the koan, an absurd question that perhaps contains the answer itself, offering a small spark of enlightenment.

THE TEST

The master asks the pupils a question to which there is no right answer. For example: What is the sound of one hand clapping? Instead of searching for the answer, the pupil must wait until the answer comes to him or her. The question becomes part of the contemplation itself.

HOW IT'S EVALUATED

When the answer finally comes, the person questioned climbs one rung higher on the ladder of enlightenment. The number of rungs to climb is not recorded. But there is usually more than one question. And so the end of one koan is the beginning of the next. The legendary dialogue between monk and master goes: 'I asked the master, "What is all this for?" He smiled and left'.

To make things even more complicated, you have to continue your daily Zen routine while working out the answer to your koan: little sleep, little food, not many warm clothes, a lot of meditation and a lot of work. The koan accompanies everything that you do. Pushed to the limits of being, it becomes a burden. Those who become engrossed in the koan break down. A considerable number of Zen monks die of the so-called Zen illness, a state of exhaustion brought on by too much contemplation.

--- GOOD TO KNOW ---

It's only when you've stopped obsessing about cracking the koan that the answer comes. The classic koan, 'Everyone has a birthplace. Where is yours?' has one possible answer: 'This morning I ate rice soup. Now I'm hungry again'. Think about it.

Here are some koans that will last you three lifetimes:

....

Stop the ship at the horizon.

A girl crosses the street.
Is she the younger or older sister?

What is half the time?

172

Will I go to heaven?

WHAT IT'S ABOUT
In many religions, life itself is a test. By what criteria is it decided whether we've passed or not?

THE TEST
At the Last Judgement, we stand before God and our lives are weighed up. Here is an overview of the world's religions.

HINDUISM
Earthly life is measured against four criteria: Karma yoga (selfless action), Bhakti yoga (religious practice and devotion), Jnana yoga (the realisation that the body is finite and the spirit is eternal) and Raja yoga (the cleansing of the mind through meditation). Depending on whether you have accumulated good or bad karma from your behaviour on earth, you enter Swarga (heaven) or Naraka (hell). But this doesn't play such an important role, because after a certain period of time in either place, atman, the eternal soul, is reborn as a plant, animal or person. This cycle of reincarnation is known as samsara ('wandering soul'). Much more important than heaven is moksha – the release from the cycles of reincarnation – a state that is beyond human comprehension, and that is so difficult to achieve that there is no description for it. But even if you are never released, it is worth leading a good life because good deeds in this life can lead to an ascent into a higher caste in the next life.

ISLAM
Those who want to enter paradise have to follow the five pillars of Islam during their lifetime: faith, prayer, the giving of alms, fasting and pilgrimage to Mecca. Alcohol and pork are also forbidden while other meat has to be ritually slaughtered. After you die, a period of waiting follows until you are resurrected on the Day of Judgement. Then each and everyone's deeds are scrutinised – good deeds have more weight than bad ones. Finally, you cross the As-Sirat Bridge that leads over hellfire to Jannah or heaven. For the god-fearing, the bridge is wide and comfortable; for sinners, it is as narrow as a hair – they fall into Jahannam, or hell. A small comfort:

Allah can lead people out of hell and back into heaven.

BUDDHISM

The cause of all suffering in the world comes from the three poisons: greed, ignorance and hatred. Only those who overcome them are enlightened and reach nirvana, a state of consciousness free of needs and dependencies. And it is reserved for the select few. Most people have to be reincarnated over and over again and have to work on their karma. You follow the 'eight-fold path': the right view, the right intentions, the right speech, the right action, the right livelihood, the right effort, the right mindfulness, and the right concentration.

JUDAISM

In the Torah, the afterlife is not mentioned at all. This doesn't mean that Jews do not believe in life after death in principle - but it's complicated. The Talmud describes heaven as a mixture of the Sabbath, sex and sunshine. But in eschatology, (the doctrine of the last things), it only plays a theological bit part. What's far more important is the Olam Ha'ba ('the world to come'). For Orthodox Jews, and for some conservatives, this is a real place; for the third largest group, the Reform

Jews, it is merely symbolic. Everyone agrees, however, that our behaviour in this life is of primary importance. Just three rules determine what may be eaten, and how - no pork, no crustaceans, no gluttony. What's important: those who live the wrong way may not count on God's mercy but may save themselves via sincere repentance and rectification.

CHRISTIANITY

In Catholicism, church attendance, communion, obeying the Ten Commandments, regular confession with an ordained priest, renunciation of meat on Fridays and an annual fortnightly fasting period are necessary but not sufficient requirements to pass the test of life. The only hope for mercy is in conjunction with religious sacraments and intercession. In Protestantism, it is sufficient to believe in God, ask for forgiveness and to recognise Jesus Christ in order to enter heaven. Protestants believe that *simul iustus et peccator* ('All men are equally just and sinners'). Only God's mercy can open the gates to heaven and, to some extent, the actions of men are irrelevant. But the doctrine of predestination also prevails: the belief that the people who are preordained for God's redemption will do good during their lifetime.

GOOD TO KNOW

The interpretation of the Holy Scriptures is naturally as complex as it is diverse: this small selection represents only a few of many possibilities.

Are we all equal?

☛ First, please do the test on the right-hand page.

THE TEST

In 1948, US psychologist Bertram Forer carried out a small experiment. He set his students a personality test and gave them a personal evaluation at the end. Then he asked his students: How applicable do you find your evaluation? On a scale from 0 to 5, students awarded themselves an average of 4.26 points. More than 80 per cent saw themselves reflected in the results.

HOW IT'S EVALUATED

In fact, the students had received exactly the same evaluation (see the text on the right). The text was a compilation of platitudes that could apply to almost anyone. Forer's experiment went down in the annals of psychological history as the Barnum Effect (named after the showman Phineas Taylor Barnum who peddled his circus with the slogan, 'Something for everyone').

The Barnum Effect applies not only to individuals, but also to companies. In 2011 Stuart Nolan asked one thousand companies to carry out a self-assessment. An evaluation containing the same profile was sent to each company: the Barnum text, adapted to company truisms. Of the 673 companies that took part, 565 (84 per cent) felt that they were either accurately or fairly accurately represented.

What does the Barnum Effect tell us? First, when we do a personality test, we clearly have a subconscious longing for the result to apply to us. Second, Barnum statements (e.g. 'You are proud of your independent way of thinking') emphasise characteristics that everyone would like to have. But the other thing we learn is that psychometric tests do not investigate individuality but highlight commonalities.

GOOD TO KNOW

Most people are not interested in finding out what they're like but want to hear that they're OK as they are: they are looking for approval, not insight.

Evaluate the extent to which the description below applies to you on a scale of 0 to 5.

You have a need for other people to like and admire you, yet you tend to be critical of yourself. While you have some personality weaknesses you are generally able to compensate for them. You have considerable unused capacity that you have not turned to your advantage. Disciplined and self-controlled on the outside, you tend to be worrisome and insecure on the inside. At times you have serious doubts as to whether you have made the right decision or done the right thing. You prefer a certain amount of change and variety and become dissatisfied when hemmed in by restrictions and limitations. You also pride yourself as an independent thinker; and do not accept others' statements without satisfactory proof. But you have found it unwise to be too frank in revealing yourself to others. At times you are extroverted, affable, and sociable, while at other times you are introverted, wary, and reserved. Some of your aspirations tend to be rather unrealistic.

does not apply at all   0 — 1 — 2 — 3 — 4 — 5   applies totally

← Now read the text on the left page.

176

Are my assumptions right?

WHAT IT'S ABOUT

Statements about the future cannot be 'right' or 'wrong': many degrees of probability lie between these two extremes. This, however, has only been common knowledge for the past three hundred years – far too short a time for our gut instincts to develop reliable intuitions with which we can judge probability.

Not only the gambling industry but also investment bankers and financial consultants live off people's inability to assess probability in a realistic manner. At least nowadays every child knows that smoking causes cancer, even though they might have a chain-smoking great-uncle in the family who lived to 95. On the basis of this kind of counter example, philosophers in the past would have refuted the hypothesis.

THE TEST

Surprisingly it was a theologian, the English Presbyterian priest Thomas Bayes, who set up the first rules for calculating probability. Thanks to him, we have the conceptual framework of 'test results', 'hypotheses' and 'background assumptions', as well as the methodology with which we can calculate the probability of hypotheses using test results. Since then nearly every test (including the ones in this book) that has been devised by ingenious scientists or psychologists is founded on his posthumously published 'Essay Towards Solving a Problem in the Doctrine of Chances' (1763).

GOOD TO KNOW

Be distrustful of anyone who tries to tell you something about risks and chances – even their own. No one can answer the following questions spontaneously and correctly. Those who can are already familiar with this kind of test.

You read that from 500,000 citizens of your age, 5,000 will contract a new type of immune deficiency that will prove fatal unless treated early. So you buy a quick prediction test that claims on the packet to be 90% reliable. Unfortunately, of 100 people who become ill, 10 cases will not be recognised by this test. And vice versa: 10 in 100 healthy people will be diagnosed falsely as ill.

How high is the probability that you are in fact suffering from the immune deficiency?

A 90%   B 81.1%   C 8.3%

☛ Turn the page for the evaluation.

The correct answer is 8.3%.

This is a classic application of the method developed by Thomas Bayes for calculating the probability of hypotheses. In the tree diagram on the right, you can see the solution. The main point is that you have to multiply the probabilities along a path in order to compute the total probability of this particular path. How high is the probability of the hypothesis that you are ill after getting an 'ill' test result? As with every probability calculation, you have to divide the number of relevant cases by the number of total possible cases. In our example this means: The probability of path 2 divided by the sum of all the paths that can lead to the 'ill' test result (path 1 plus path 2).

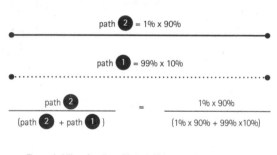

The probability of an 'I am ill' result if the test showed 'ill': 8.3%

Although a test result of 8.3% probability may seem surprisingly low, it would be rash to give the all-clear. That's because this result also means that you have an 8.3 times higher probability than the (untested) people in your age group, who only have a 1% probability of being ill. Or, to put it more dramatically: you are 830% more likely to have an immune deficiency than others.

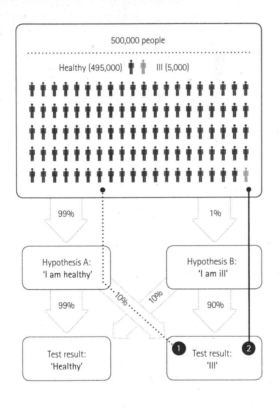

Appendix

TEST THEORY

Item

The individual tasks of a test are called 'items'.

Likert scale

A symmetric scale of answers to an item, mostly: (1) strongly disagree, (2) disagree, (3) neither agree nor disagree, (4) agree, (5) strongly agree.

Social desirability bias

When, especially in psychological tests, respondents falsify their answers because they know either consciously or subconsciously what the test administrator wants to hear, this is referred to as social desirability bias. The most famous example of this is playing down alcohol consumption.

Culturally stable

A test is culturally stable when the family background of the test respondent has no relevant influence on the test results.

Construct

Intelligence, creativity and personality are not truths but abstract, theoretical and therefore debatable constructs.

Standardised test

If a test is based on a unified testing system that fulfils the quality criteria of objectivity, reliability and validity, it is 'standardised'.

Objectivity

This describes whether the result of a testing system is free from random boundary constraints. An example of this is when the test respondent's positive or negative feelings towards the test administrator have no influence on the test result. In short: Do test administrator A and B achieve the same result with the same test respondent?

Reliability

This describes how stable a measurement result is if the test is carried out several times under the same objective circumstances. It is a degree of the test's accuracy of measurement: How strongly are the test results subject to purely random distribution?

Validity

This describes whether the test truly measures what it is supposed to measure. An intelligence test that lacks validity only says something about the capability of measuring intelligence test questions – but nothing about what we have defined as 'intelligence'.

Ceiling effect and floor effect

These are measurement errors that occur when the test questions are either too easy or too difficult. With test respondents who answer everything correctly, it is impossible to work out who would have scored better than the others, had the questions been more difficult (ceiling effect). By contrast, a test has no validity in terms of individual differentiation if none of the test respondents is able to answer any of the questions correctly (floor effect). The formulation of test questions has to cover the entire spectrum in order to get the most informative result possible.

Normal distribution

Every characteristic (of nature, people or test results) that does not have an absolutely precise value is distributed around an average value according to the law of chance. This completely random (in other words, not individual) distribution has a distribution curve that resembles a bell and was first described in mathematical terms by German mathematician Carl Friedrich Gauß – the so-called 'normal distribution'. The standard deviation represents the extent of deviation from the norm. If you want to know how good you are in comparison to the (normally distributed) entire population, you have to ask: How many standard deviations do I lie above or below the average? It is not that we do well or badly in tests, but in comparison to other answers, we do averagely, below averagely or above averagely.

Norm group

In order for a child to avoid comparing him- or herself with the above average, the individual test results are compared to a specific section of the entire population, the norm group.

Specificity and sensitivity

The sensitivity of a diagnostic test describes how many truly ill people are correctly diagnosed by a particular test. The specificity of a test indicates how many healthy people it identifies as healthy.

SOURCES

184 ☛ In alphabetical order

The Afterlife Test
Krogerus, Mikael: 'Reiseführer in den Himmel', in: *DUMMY* Magazin, issue 40.

The Age Test
Chuard, Claude: 'Zur Geschichte der Sterbetafeln', http://izs.napoleon.ch/upload/dokumente/Hist_Sterbetafeln.pdf, accessed on 01.05.2014.
German data: https://www.destatis.de
Austrian data: http://www.statistik.at
Swiss data: http://www.bfs.admin.ch
Mortality table data © Statistisches Bundesamt, Wiesbaden 2013, Reproduction and distribution, also of excerpts, are permitted provided that the source is mentioned. Test life expectancy online: http://symptomat.de/online-test/wie_alt_werde_ich.php?data=true

The Alcoholic Test
Babor, T., Higgins-Biddle, J., Saunders, J., Monteiro, M.: AUD IT. *The Alcohol Use Disorders Identification Test. Guideline for Use in Primary Care*, World Health Organization WHO, Geneva 2001. See also: http://whqlibdoc.who.int/hq/2001/WHO_MSD_MSB_01.6a.pdf, accessed on 10.06.2014.

The Attention Test
The original d2 test was developed by R. Brickenkamp. Brickenkamp, R., Schmidt-Atzert, L, Liepmann, D.: *Test d2 – Revision (d2-R). Aufmerksamkeits- und Konzentrationstest*, Göttingen: Hogrefe 2010.

The Ayurveda Test
Murray, Angela H.: *Ayurveda for Dummies*, Chichester 2013.
Various constitution tables including: http://www.banyanbotanicals.com/constitutions/, http://www.ayurveda-portal.de/ayurveda-wissen/ayurveda-einfuehrung/ayurveda-konstitutionstabelle. html#.U5TYD sdEP84, http://doshaquiz.chopra.com/, accessed on 01.06.2014.

The Barnum Effect
Forer, Bertram R.: 'The Fallacy of Personal Validation. A Classroom Demonstration of Gullibility', in: *The Journal of Abnormal Psychology*, 44, 1949, p. 118–121.
Nolan, Stuart: TEDxSalford, http://youtube/3Ls-9lx_JtuM, accessed on 13.05.2014.

The Bayesian Estimation
Gigerenzer, Gerd: *Risiko. Wie man die richtigen Entscheidungen trifft*, Munich 2013. http://de.wikipedia.org/wiki/Gigerenzer

The Bechdel Test

http://bechdeltest.com
http://therepresentationproject.org
The table shown is an abbreviated
version of the table by Daniel Mariani.
Among other interesting graphs
('Visualizing the Bechdel Test') it can be
found at: www.tenchocolatesundaes.
blogspot.com.br

The Big Five Test

Gosling, S. D.: *Snoop. What Your Stuff
Says About You*, London 2008.
Gosling, S. D., Rentfrow, P. J., Swann, W.
B., Jr.: 'A Very Brief Measure of the Big
Five Personality Domains', in: *Journal of
Research in Personality*, 37, 2013,
p. 504–528. See also: http://homepage.
psy.utexas.edu/HomePage/Faculty/
Gosling/ scales_we.htm, accessed on
01.06.2014. Norm distribution with the
kind permission of Jason Rentfrow,
University of Cambridge, Department of
Psychology.
Ostendorf, F., Angleitner, A.:
*NEO-Persönlichkeitsinventar nach Costa
and McCrae*. Revised edition (NEO-PI-R),
Göttingen: Hogrefe 2004.

The Body Mass Index

Interview with Katherine Flegal:
'Katherine Flegal Discusses the
Prevalence of Obesity in the US',
http://archive.sciencewatch.com/ana/st/
obesity2/10sepObes2Fleg/, accessed on
30.05.2014.
Intelligent BMI calculator: http://
de.smartbmicalculator.com, accessed on
11.06.2014.

The Clock Test

Kørner, Ejnar Alex, Lauritzen, Lise,
Mørkeberg Nilsson, Flemming, Lolk,
Annette, Christensen, Peder: 'Simple
Scoring of the Clock-Drawing Test for
Dementia Screening', in: *Danish Medical
Journal*, 59, 2012, http://www.danmedj.
dk/portal/page/portal/danmedj.dk/
dmj_forside/PAST_ISSUE/2012/
DMJ_2012_01/A4365, accessed on
30.05.2014.
Alzheimer's in the News: http://
www.nhs.uk/news/2011/08August/
Documents/Alzheimer's%20in%20
the%20press.pdf, accessed on
01.06.2014.

The Cooper Test

Cooper, K. H.: 'A means of assessing
maximal oxygen uptake', in: *Journal of
the American Medical Association*, 203,
1968, p. 201–204.

The Copy Test

Seibt, Constantin: *Deadline. Wie man
besser schreibt*, Zurich 2013.
http://www.economist.com/styleguide,
accessed on 14.05.2014.

The Core Self-Evaluation Test

Judge, T.A., Erez, A., Bono, J.E., Thoresen,
C.J.: 'The core self-evaluation scale:
Development of a measure' in:
Personnel Psychology, 56/2, 2003.

The Creativity Test

Beilock, S. L., Carr, T. H.: 'On the Fragility
of Skilled Performance. What Governs
Choking Under Pressure?', in: *Journal of
Experimental Psychology*, 130/4, 2001,

p. 701–725.

Dippo, Caitlin: 'Evaluating The Alternative Uses Test of Creativity', http://www.ncurproceedings.org/ojs/index.php/NCUR 2013/article/viewFile/547/346, accessed on 31.05.2014.

Jarosz, A. F., Colflesh, G. J. H, Wiley, J.: 'Uncorking the Muse. Alcohol Intoxication Facilitates Creative Problem Solving', in: *Consciousness and Cognition*, 21, 2012, p. 487–493.

Munro, John: 'Insights into the Creativity Process. Identifying and Measuring Creativity', https://students.education.unimelb.edu.au/selage/pub/readings/creativity UTC_Assessing__creativity_.pdf, accessed on 31.05.2014.

The Discrimination Test
The 'Rejection Sensitivity-Race Scale' was conceived for Afro-Americans, so the results cannot be compared with the European context. Nevertheless, the questions can be helpful in considering the experience of discrimination. The full questionnaire and study can be accessed at the website of the institute: http://socialrelations.psych.columbia.edu.

Gladwell, Malcolm: *Blink: The Power of Thinking Without Thinking*, London 2006.

Mendoza-Denton, R., Downey, G., Purdie, V., Davis, A.: 'Sensitivity to Race-Based Rejection. Implications for African-American Students' College Experience', in: *Journal of Personality and Social Psychology*, 83, 2002, p. 896–918.

Tierny, John: 'A Shocking Test of Bias', http://tierneylab.blogs.nytimes.com/2008/11/18/a-shocking-test-of-bias/?_php=true&_type=blogs&_r=0, accessed on 01.05.2014.

The EQ Test
Goleman, Daniel: *EQ. Emotionale Intelligenz*, Munich 2001.

Illouz, Eva: *Die Errettung der modernen Seele. Therapien, Gefühle und die Kultur der Selbsthilfe*, Frankfurt am Main 2011.

Mayer, J. D., Salovey, P., Caruso, D. R.: 'Emotional Intelligence. Theory, Findings, and Implications', in: *Psychology Inquiry*, 15/3, 2004. See also: http://www.calcasa.org/wp-content/uploads/files/ei2004mayersaloveycarusotarget.pdf, accessed on 09.03.2014.

Vasek, Thomas, *Inflation der Anerkennung*, http://www.brandeins.de/archiv/2011/respekt/inflation-deranerkennung.html, accessed on 23.02.2014.

The Familiarity Test
Gosling, Sam: *Snoop*, London 2008.

Nathanson, Craig, Williams, Kevin M., Paulhus, Delroy L: *The Diagnostic Value of Academic and Music Knowledge for Estimating Cognitive Ability and Narcissism*, University of British Columbia. See also: http://neuron4.psych.ubc.ca/~dellab/research/oct.html, accessed on 30.05.2014.

The Fear of Missing Out Test
Przybylski, A. K., Murayama, K., DeHaan, C. R., Gladwell, V.: 'Motivational, emotional, and behavioral correlates of fear of missing out', in: *Computers*

in Human Behavior, 29, 2013,
p.1814–1848. See also: http://www.
andrewprzybylski.me/resources/2013_
FearofMissingOut.pdf, accessed on
31.05.2014.
Turkle, Sherry: *Alone Together. Why We
Expect More from Technology and Less
from Each Other*, New York 2013.

The Feng Shui Test
Isemann, Thomas (feng shui advisor):
Interview with the authors on
15.03.2014.

The Four-Question Partnership Test
Fromm, Erich: *Die Kunst des Liebens*,
Berlin 1989.
Palmen, Connie: 'Letzte Fragen', in: *Das
Magazin*, 51, 2005.

The German Test
Fletcher, Adam: *How to Be German in 50
Easy Steps*, Munich 2013.

The GMAT
Yeaple, Ronald: 'MBA Play',
http://www.forbes.com/sites/
ronaldyeaple/2012/08/06/what-
thegmat-doesnt-predict/, accessed on
13.06.2014.
GMAT-Scoreboard: http://
poetsandquants.com/2014/01/04/
why-53-countries-beat-the-us-on-the-
gmat/2/
Brunner, Simon, Kemming, Jan-Dirk:
Interview with the authors.

The Graphology Test
Känzig, Rudolf: *Grafologie. Menschen
anhand ihrer Schrift verstehen und
beurteilen*, Munich 1991.
Klages, Ludwig: *Handschrift und
Charakter. Gemeinverständlicher Abriß
der graphologischen Technik*, Bonn
1989.
Recommendations from the
International Graphoanalysis Society at
www.igas.com

The Handedness Test
Oldfield, R. C.: 'The Assessment and
Analysis of Handedness. The Edinburgh
Inventory', *Neuropsychologia*, 9, 1971,
p. 97–113.
Seynsche, Monika: 'Die falsche Hand
und das richtige Hirn', http://www.
deutschlandfunk.de/die-falsche-
hand-und-das-richtige-hirn.740.
de.html?dram:article_id=111557,
accessed on 01.06.14.
Test based on Edinburgh Handedness
Inventory (Revised): Williams, Dr.
Stephen M., Colchester, Version 1.1,
http://homepage.ntlworld.com/steve.
williams7/A%20major%20revision%20
of%20the%20Edinburgh%20
Handedness%20Inventory.pdf, accessed
on 30.05.2014.

The Iced Water Test
Moreira Tiplt, Ana Lúcia:
*Schmerztherapie und Akupunktur.
Eine interkulturelle Begegnung am
Beispiel einer interdisziplinären
Schmerzambulanz*, Munich 2010. See
also: http://edoc.ub.uni-muenchen.
de/12032/1/Tiplt_Ana_Lucia.pdf,
accessed on 01.06.2014.

The IQ Test

Enzensberger, Hans Magnus: 'Im Irrgarten der Intelligenz. Über den getesteten Verstand und den Unverstand des Testens', *Neue Zürcher Zeitung* from 11.11.2006, http://www.nzz.ch/aktuell/startseite/articleEN2QA-1.74794, accessed on 01.06.2014.

Gürtler, Detlef: *Wir sind Elite. Das Bildungswunder*, Gütersloh 2009.

Modern IQ Ranges for Various Occupations: http://www.iqcomparisonsite.com/occupations.aspx, abgerufen am 30.06.2014.

The Job Test

Hossiep, R., Paschen, M.: *Bochumer Inventar zur berufsbezogenen Persönlichkeitsbeschreibung. 2.*, completely revised edition (BIP). Göttingen: Hogrefe 2003.

Ware; Bronnie: *5 Dinge, die Sterbende am meisten bereuen. Einsichten, die Ihr Leben verändern werden*, Munich 2013.

The Job Interview Test

Bryant, Adam: 'In Head-Hunting, Big Data May Not Be Such a Big Deal', Interview mit Laszlo Bock, http://www.nytimes.com/2013/06/20/business/in-head-hunting-big-data-may-not-besuch-a-big-deal.html, abgerufen am 27.05.2014.

Friedman, Thomas L.: 'How to Get a Job at Google', http://www.nytimes.com/2014/02/23/opinion/sunday/friedman-how-to-get-a-job-atgoogle.html, accessed on 01.06.2014.

The Koan Test

Faure, Bernard: *The Rhetoric of Immediacy. A Cultural Critique of Zen*, Princeton 1994.

Merton, Thomas: *Mystics and Zen Masters*, New York 1967.

Takada, Yoshihito: *Talking About Buddhism*, Tokyo 1997.

Watts, Alan W.: *The Way of Zen*, New York 1957.

Yamada, Mumon: *How to Practice Zazen*, Kyoto, Institute for Zen Studies.

The Lateralisation Test

McGilchrist, Iain: *The Master and His Emissary. The Divided Brain and the Making of the Western World*, New Haven / London 2012. See also: https://www.ted.com/talks/iain_mcgilchrist_the_divided_brain, http://www.telegraph.co.uk/news/good-toshare/10515373/Are-you-right-brained-or-leftbrained.html

Brugger, Peter: Conversation with the authors on 14.05.2014 in Zurich.

The Leadership Test

Neubauer, A. C., Bergner, S., Felfe, J.: *Leadership Judgement Indicator (LJI). Deutschsprachige Adaptation des Leadership Judgement Indicator (LJI)* von Michael Lock und Robert Wheeler, Bern 2012.

Lotter, Wolf: 'Goodbye, Johnny', in: *brandeins*, vol. 02/2006, http://www.brandeins.de/archiv/2006/leadership/goodbye-johnny.html, accessed on 15.05.2014.

http://www.formula4leadership.com, accessed on 23.05.2015.

The Learning Type Test

www.vark-learn.com

www.wikihow.com/Learn

The Lie Detector Test

Inbau, Fred E., Reid, John E., Buckley, Joseph P., Jayne, Brian C.: *Essentials Of The Reid Technique. Criminal Interrogation and Confessions*, Burlington 2013.

Kroll, Ottmar, 'Reid®-Methode', http://www.krimlex.de/artikel. php?BUCHSTABE=&KL_ID=224, accessed on 14.05.2014.

Starr, Douglas: 'The Interview', http://archives.newyorker.com/?i=2013-12-09#folio=042, accessed on 14.05.2014.

Volyk, Andriy: 'History of the Polygraph', http://www.wikihow.com/Cheat-a-Polygraph-Test-(Lie-Detector), accessed on 01.06.2014.

History of the Polygraph: http://www.argo-a.com.ua/eng/history.html, accessed on 14.05.2014.

The Maximisation Test

Gross, Peter: Die Multioptionsgesellschaft, Frankfurt am Main 1994.

Nenkov, G. Y., Morrin, M., Ward, A., Schwartz, B., Hulland, J.: 'A short form of the Maximization Scale. Factor structure, reliability and validity studies', in: *Judgment and Decision Making*, Volume 3/5, 2008.

The Mirror Test

Nemitz, Rolf: http://lacan-entziffern.de

Rouge-Test: http://medlibrary.org/medwiki/Rouge_test

The Myers–Briggs Type Indicator

Gladwell, Malcolm: 'Personality Plus', http://www.newyorker.com/archive/2004/09/20/040920fa_fact_gladwell, accessed on 02.05.2014.

Myers, I. B., McCaulley, M. H., Quenk, N. L, Hammer, A. L.: MBTI Manual. *A Guide to the Development and Use of the Myers-Briggs Type Indicator*, Mountain View 1998.

Paul, Annie Murphy: *The Cult of Personality Testing. How Personality Tests Are Leading Us to Miseducate Our Children, Mismanage Our Companies, and Misunderstand Ourselves*, New York 2005.

The Narcissism Test

Cheek, J. M., Hendin, H. M., Wink., P. M.: *An Extended Version of the Hypersensitive Narcissism Scale*, June Posters 2013.

Kaufman, Scott Barry: '23 Signs You're Secretly a Narcissist Masquerading as a Sensitive Introvert', http://blogs.scientificamerican.com/beautiful-minds/2013/08/26/23-signs-youre-secretly-a-narcissist-masquerading-as-a-sensitive-introvert/, accessed on 11.06.2014.

Lasch, Christopher, *Das Zeitalter des Narzissmus*, Munich 1982.

Maaz, Hans-Joachim: *Die narzisstische Gesellschaft*. Ein Psychogramm, Munich 2012.

The Oxbridge Test

Farndon, John: *Do You Think You're Clever?* The Oxford and Cambridge Questions, London 2010.

The Parents' Test

Bowles, Colin: *The Beginner's Guide to Fatherhood. What to Do, When You Haven't a Clue*, Skyview 2012.

Parsons, Rob: *The Sixty Minute Father. How Time Well Spent Can Change Your Child's Life Forever*, London 1996.

Rosin, Hanna: 'The Overprotected Kid', http://www.theatlantic.com/features/archive/2014/03/hey-parents-leave-those-kids-alone/358631/,accessed on 01.06.2014.

The Politics Test

Politicalcompass.org
EUandi.eu
Smartvorte.ch

The Psychopath Test

Chivers, Tom: 'Psychopaths. How can You Spot one?', http://www.telegraph.co.uk/culture/books/10737827/Psychopaths-how-can-youspot-one.html, accessed on 13.05.2014.

Hare, Robert: *Without Conscience: The Disturbing World of the Psychopaths Amongst Us, 1999.*

Miller, Gregg: 'What It's Like to Spend 20 Years Listening to Psychopaths for Science', Interview with Kent Kiehl, http://www.wired.com/2014/04/psychopath-brains-kiehl/?mbid=social_fb, accessed on 23.05.2014.

Stout, Martha: *The Sociopath Next Door*, New York, 2006.

PCL-R: https://en.wikipedia.org/wiki/Hare_Psychopathy_Checklist

The Push-Up Test

Coburn, Jared W., Malek, Moh H.: NSCA's *Essentials of Personal Training*, Champaign 2012.

Golding, L. A. et al.: *Y's Way to Physical Fitness. The Complete Guide to Fitness Testing and Instruction*, Champaign 1986.

Hoffmann, Jay: *Norms for Fitness, Performance, and Health*, Champaign 2006.

McArdle, W. D. et al: *Essentials of Exercise Physiology*, Philadelphia 2006.

Niemann, D. C.: *Exercise Testing and Perscription. A Health Related Approach*, Mountain View 1999.

How to Do More Push-Ups: http://www.youtube.com/watch?v=AtGqLm9HDSU, accessed on 01.06.2014.

The Reading Test

www.spritzinc.com

The Risk Test

Ferber, Michael: *Was Sie über Geldanlage wissen sollten. Ein Wegweiser der Neuen Zürcher Zeitung für Privatanleger*, Zurich 2012.

Jörg Perrin, Petra: *Geschlechts-und ausbildungsspezifische Unterschiede im Investitionsverhalten*, Bern 2007.

Niedermayer, Daniel, Wagner, Marcel: *Exchange Traded Funds und Anlagestrategien*, Zurich 2012.

The Rorschach Test

Burstein, Alvin G., Loucks, Sandra: *Rorschach's Test. Scoring and Interpretation*, New York 1989.

Exner, John E. Jr: *Rorschach-*

Arbeitsbuch für das Comprehensive System. German version of 'A Rorschach Workbook for the Comprehensive System – Fifth Edition', translated by Irmgard Slanar. Bern: Verlag Hans Huber, 2010.

The Ruler Test
Marieb, Elaine N.: *Human Anatomy and Physiology*, San Francisco 2003.

The School Test
Onion, Rebecca: 'Test Your Kids' Knowledge Against the Well-Informed Children of 1930', http://www.slate.com/blogs/the_vault/2013/10/25/information_test_written_to_assess_children_in_1930.html, accessed on 30.05.2014.

The Self-Leadership-Test
Adapted from Houghton, J. D., Dawley, D., DiLiello, T. C.: 'The Abbreviated Self-Leadership Questionnaire (ASLQ): A More Concise Measure of Self-Leadership', in: *International Journal of Leadership Studies*, 7, 2012, p. 216–232. The German version of the RSLQ, and the long version of the ASLQ can be found online at: http://www.uni-kiel.de/psychologie/AOM/index.php/self-leadership-questionnaire.html

The Senses Test
Neckel, Sighard: 'Erfolg', in: Bröckling, Ulrich, Krasmann, Susanne, Lemke, Thomas (Eds.): *Glossar der Gegenwart*, Frankfurt am Main 2004, p. 63–70. Robinson, Ken: *Finding Your Element*, New York 2013.

Schrupp, Antje: 'Im Bezugsgewebe menschlicher Angelegenheiten', http://www.antjeschrupp.de/im-bezugsgewebe-menschlicher-angelegenheiten, accessed on 01.06.2014.

The Sex Test
Hudson, W. W.: The WALMYR Assessment Scales Scoring Manual. Tallahassee, FL, WALMYR Publishing Co. 1992, www.walmyr.com, Copyright © 1992, Walter W. Hudson.

The Sight Test
The Foundation of the American Academy of Ophthalmology: 'Herman Snellen', http://museumofvision.org/dynamic/files/uploaded_files_filename_157.pdf, accessed on 30.05.2014.

The Sit and Reach Test
Robbins, Gwen, Powers, Debbie, Burgess, Sharon: *A wellness way of life*, New York 2004.
Backscratch: http://www.topendsports.com/testing/tests/shoulder-flexibility.htm, accessed on 02.04.2014.

The Stork Test
Johnson, B. L., Nelson, J. K.: *Practical Measurements for Evaluation in Physical Education*, Minneapolis 1979.
Mackenzie, B.: 'Standing Stork Test', http://www.brianmac.co.uk/storktst.htm, accessed on 22.05.2014.
Norm table: Schell, J., Leelarthaepin, B.: *Physical Fitness Assessment in Exercise and Sports Science*, Leelar

Biomedisience Services, Matraville 1994, p. 327.

Comparative study of standing on one leg and the risk of injury: Wyss, T., Roos, L., Wunderlin, S., Mäder, U.: 'Comparison of Two Balance Tests to Predict Injury Risk in a Military Setting', in: Book of Abstracts, 17th Congress of the European College of Sport Science, Brussels 2012, p. 605.

The Stress Test

Levitan, Sar A., Gallo, Frank: 'Work and Family. The Impact of Legislation', *Monthly Labour Review*, March 1990, http://www.bls.gov/opub/mlr/1990/03/art5full.pdf, accessed on 31.05.2014.
Maslach, Christina; Jackson, Susan E.: 'The Measurement of Experienced Burnout', in: *Journal of occupational behaviour*, Bd. 2, 1981, p. 99–113, http://onlinelibrary.wiley.com/doi/10.1002/job.4030020205/pdf, accessed on 31.05.2014.
Parakati, Vania: 'The History of Work/Life Balance. It's Not as New as You Think', 2010, http://www.examiner.com/article/the-history-of-work-life-balance-its-not-as-new-as-you-think-1, abgerufen am 31.05.2014.
Wheeler, Kevin: 'Figuring Out Work-Life Balance', 2007, http://www.ere.net/2007/01/11/figuring-out-work-life-balance/, accessed on 31.05.2014.

The Subjective Happiness Scale

Lyubomirsky, Sonja: *Glücklich sein. Warum Sie es in der Hand haben, zufrieden zu leben*, Frankfurt am Main 2008.

Normierung: Lyubomirsky, S., Lepper, H.: 'A Measure of Subjective Happiness. Preliminary Reliability and Construct Validation', in: *Social Indicators Research*, 46, 1999, p. 137–155, http://sonjalyubomirsky.com/wp-content/themes/sonjalyubomirsky/papers/LL1999.pdf, accessed on 17.06.2014. See also: http://sonjalyubomirsky.com
Rubin, Gretchen: *Das Happiness-Projekt. Oder: Wie ich ein Jahr damit verbrachte, mich um meine Freunde zu kümmern, den Kleiderschrank auszumisten, Philosophen zu lesen und überhaupt mehr Freude am Leben zu haben*, Frankfurt am Main 2011.

The Temperament Test

Asendorpf, Jens B., Meyer, Franz J.: *Psychologie der Persönlichkeit*, Berlin 2012.
Littauer, Florence: *Einfach typisch! Die vier Temperamente unter der Lupe*, Aßlar 2002.

The Teutonic Test

Fletcher, Adam: *How to be German in Fifty Easy Steps*, Munich 2013

The Turing Test

Marcus, Gary: 'Why Can't My Computer Understand Me?', The *New Yorker* from 16.08.2013, http://www.newyorker.com/online/blogs/elements/2013/08/why-cant-my-computer-understand-me.html, abgerufen am 30.05.2014.
Pietsch, Katharina: 'Ridley Scott's Blade Runner' (1982)', http://www.ruhr-uni-bochum.de/philosophy/didaktik_kultur/

pdf/TexteUtopie/Blade%20Runner.pdf, accessed on 30.05.2014.

The Two-Question Depression Test
Whooley, Mary A., Avins, Andrew L., Miranda, Jeanne, Browner, Warren S.: 'Case-Finding Instruments for Depression. Two Questions Are as Good as Many', in: Journal of General Internal Medicine, July 1997, p. 439–445, http://www.ncbi.nlm.nih.gov/pmc/articles/PMC1497134/, accessed on 30.05.2014.
Kroenke, K., Spitzer, R. L., Williams, J. B., Monahan, P. O., Löwe, B.: 'Anxiety disorders in primary care: prevalence impairment, comorbidity, and detection', in: Annals of Internal Medicine, 2007.

The Vertical Jump Test
Arkinstall, M. et al.: *Macmillan VCE Physical Education 2*, Malaysia 2010.
Briggs, Marc: *Training for Soccer Players*, Ramsbury 2013.
Hoffman, Jay: *Norms for Fitness, Performance, and Health*, Champaign 2006.
Normed Jump Test table: http://www.topendsports.com/testing/norms/vertical-jump.htm, accessed on 18.06.2014.

The Wealth Test
Druyen, Thomas, Lauterbach, Wolfgang, Grundmann, Matthias (Hrsg.): *Reichtum und Vermögen. Zur gesellschaftlichen Bedeutung der Reichtumsund Vermögensforschung*, Wiesbaden 2009.
Firebaugh, Glenn, Tach, Laura: 'Income and Happiness in the United States', 2004, http://citation.allacademic.com/meta/p_mla_apa_research_citation/0/1/8/1/6/pages18167/p18167-1.php, accessed on 31.05.2014.
Exciting comparisons of wealth: www.globalrichlist.com

The WpM Test
Mueller, Pam A., Oppenheimer, Daniel M.: 'The Pen Is Mightier Than the Keyboard. Advantages of Longhand Over Laptop Note Taking', *Psychological Science*, April 2014, http://www.academia.edu/6273095/The_Pen_Is_Mightier_Than_The_Keyboard_Advantages_of_Longhand_Over_Laptop_Note_Taking, abgerufen am 18.06.2014.
Deutscher Stenografenbund: www.stenografenbund.de
How to type faster: http://hackmystudy.com/how_to_type_faster_free.html

ACKNOWLEDGEMENTS

194 Our first thanks go to Ulrich Kühne who checked our tests vigilantly and constructively as well as writing the Bayesian Estimation test himself. The koan chapter was contributed by Michaela Vieser, and the IQ and gene test were written by Detlef Gürtler.

We thank Jürgen Mohn (University of Basel) for his suggestion that life itself is a test. Mirko Derpmann was, as always, a valuable prompter. Kai Michel took us on a short excursion into Biblical history and Rebecca Lämmle into the nature of oracles. Markus Ferrer and Jacqueline Klauser analysed our handwriting. Dr. Sam Gosling (Texas University) honed our view of the Big Five. Ueli Tschäppeler advised us on body fat and girth size issues. Dr. Mirko Schmidt (University of Bern) scrutinised the sporting performance tests. Dr. Eugen Häni supplied us with depression and dementia tests. Susan T. Fiske (Princeton University) opened our eyes to social-political tests. Hans Diem analysed us with the aid of Rorschach tables, Thomas Isemann initiated us into the mysteries of feng shui, and Andre Wantz (University of Bern) explained how our brains work. Jeff Buckley from John E. Reid Associates gave us an introduction into the nature of interrogation. Simon Brunner, Jan-Dirk Kemming, Benno Maggi and Franziska Schutzbach were wonderful sparring partners. Thanks to Dr. G.-Jürgen Hogrefe for the Rorschach tables, d2, BIP and LJI.

We are extremely grateful to all the scientists who gave us permission to use their tests: Myrna Hudson (ISS), Stephan Elspaß (Atlas der deutschen Alltagssprache) Jonathan Cheek (MCNS), Alexander H. Trechsel (EU Profiler) Jason Rentfrow and Sam Gosling (TIPI), Jeffrey D. Houghton (ASLQ), the WHO (AUDIT), Sonja Lyubomirsky (SHS), Barry Schwarz (MS), Delroy L. Paulhus (OCQ), Thaddeus Stephens (MBTI®), Neil D. Fleming (VARK®), Adam Fletcher (How German am I?). And we give thanks to Evan Forsch for what is probably the truest personality test: the toothpaste personality test.

Patrick Sielemann prevented mistakes and filled in the best parts of the manuscript. Carla Schmid designed checkbox after checkbox with poise, Lisa Mühlemann diligently and successfully took care of licences, and Peter Haag gave us his full trust (again) without qualification. Michael 'allow it' Bhaskar: thank you very much for the pints. We are indebted to Viola Zimmerman, Sven Weber, Juliane Wolski and Chantal Meg for the fantastic layout designs.

The Test Book was tested by: Oliver Ferilli, Michael Rüegger, Barbara Rolli and Thomas Ehrlich.

Finally we would like to thank Cédric Hiltbrand, lic.phil. psychologist. He works as a test expert for the Testzentrale Hogrefe in Bern. There is probably no other Swiss person who has undergone more tests than he has. He opened up new doors in the world of psychodiagnostics.

THE AUTHORS

MIKAEL KROGERUS

Cooper Test (12-minute run): 3,000 metres, very good. Emotional intelligence (MSCEIT™): 112. Two-Question Depression Test: not depressed. MBTI®: ENFP (enthusiastic and resourceful but also needs a great deal of encouragement). Social media addiction: pronounced. Handedness: ambidextrous. Ayurveda constitution: vata.

ROMAN TSCHÄPPELER

IQ (logical thinking, IST2000): 119. Leadership style: directive. Attention test: impulsive. Push-up test: 36 (good). MBTI®: ESTJ (does everything right but unfortunately expects others to do so too). Feng shui test: 8 points (very good). Risk test: balanced investment strategy. BMI: 26.8.

NOTES

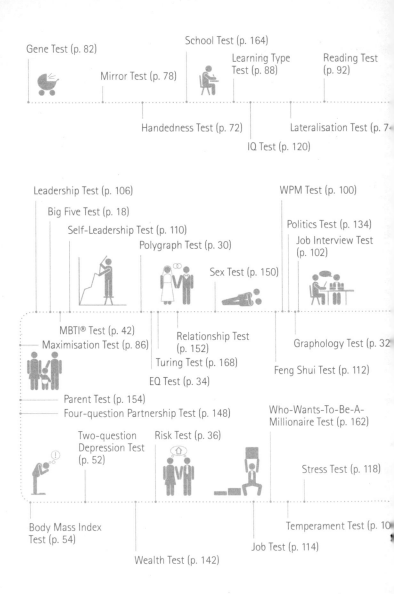